DIE WITH MEMORIES, NOT JUST DREAMS

TAKE 7 POWERFUL ACTIONS
TO CREATE YOUR OWN CASTLES

ROB SPERRY

DIE WITH MEMORIES, NOT JUST DREAMS

TAKE 7 POWERFUL ACTIONS
TO CREATE YOUR OWN CASTLES

ROB SPERRY

TGON Publishing

TGON Publishing

Copyright © 2024 Rob Sperry

All rights reserved

No part of this book may be reproduced in any form or by any electronic or mechanical means including information storage and retrieval systems, without permission in writing from the author. The only exception is by a reviewer, who may quote short excerpts in a published review.

The information presented herein represents the views of the author as of the date of publication. This book is presented for informational purposes only. While every attempt has been made to verify the information in this book, the author does not assume any responsibility for errors, inaccuracies, or omissions.

CONTENTS

FOREWORD	9
PREFACE	13
INTRODUCTION	23

1 CLARIFY WHAT YOU WANT — 27

- **ACTION 1:** DREAM AND CRAFT A CLEAR VISION
- **ACTION 2:** BELIEVE IN THE INEVITABILITY OF SUCCESS
- **ACTION 3:** PICK YOUR TOP PRIORITIES

2 BUILD MOMENTUM — 83

- **ACTION 4:** TAKE ACTION AND MASTER THE MINIMUMS
- **ACTION 5:** CREATE AND CELEBRATE WIN STREAKS
- **ACTION 6:** CREATE A SUPPORTIVE ENVIRONMENT

3 SUSTAIN SUCCESS — 141

- **ACTION 7:** DEFEAT DEMONS/ DISTRACTIONS WITH DISCIPLINE

AFTERWORD	180
ABOUT THE AUTHOR	185

Make the most of your time and life.

– Hal Elrod

FOREWORD

MOVE INTO YOUR CASTLES

You and I want the same things: a healthy body, a good life, a happy home, rewarding family relationships, and a prosperous profession or thriving business.

These are what Rob Sperry calls "castles." His book will help you design, build, and move into yours–one stone or step at a time–by taking simple, consistent actions.

Rob shows you how you can dream big and then take small steps forward, gaining confidence and maintaining momentum even while starting a winning streak!

That's why I am alive today. At age twenty, my life ended when my car was hit head-on by a drunk driver. I actually died for six minutes, broke eleven bones, suffered permanent brain damage, and was told by doctors that I would never walk again. And yet, I remained positive–so positive that my doctors thought I must be in denial.

Defying the temptation to be a victim, I miraculously took my first step just three weeks after being found dead and told I would never walk again. Not only did I walk, I eventually ran a fifty-two-mile ultra-marathon. I also became a hall of fame business achiever, an international keynote speaker, a bestselling author, and–most importantly–a husband and a father.

My near-death experience taught me the importance of leading life one moment, one day, one morning, at a time. Life is such a precious gift, and it's so sad and tragic to see a life wasted and filled with regrets when we could be creating many beautiful memories day by day.

I often ask people: What if you could miraculously wake up tomorrow and any–or every–area of your life was transformed? What would be different? Would you be happier? Healthier? More successful? In better shape? Would you have more energy? Less stress? More money? Better relationships? Which of your problems would be solved?

You may believe that anything is possible. Yet "possible" isn't enough to get you out of bed in the morning fueled with the internal clarity and motivation to tackle your biggest dreams. As Rob and I can attest: You need to move your vision of success, your "dream castles," from possible... to probable... to inevitable. How? With unwavering faith and extraordinary effort, maintaining specific minimal daily disciplines.

In this book, Rob coaches us on how to start making progress. He and I know from experience that seeing how much progress you've made is one of the most empowering, confidence-inspiring, and enjoyable experiences that can't be duplicated any other way.

There are countless self-help and leadership books that provide us with useful tips, but very few clearly spell out what we need to believe, be, and do to achieve the results we want.

What strategies, mindsets, rituals, practices, and systems do peak performers maintain daily to get to the top and stay there? The more we study the top people in any industry, the more we realize that their success is a result of who they are, not just what they do.

We're all striving to get to the next level of personal and professional success. We all want to take our lives, our businesses, and ourselves to the next level. You first figure out how to take yourself to the next level and that's exactly what this book will help you do. With Rob's coaching you can get there, faster than you ever thought possible, simply by "Mastering the Minimums" as he calls our non-negotiable commitments.

Rob shares several personal stories and stories from the lives of other successful people to show how the demands of their profession sometimes left them stressed, overweight, and unfulfilled. They experienced many failures, but they persisted believing in their dreams. They imagined their dream castles, and eventually they engineered them and moved into them.

You can, too! Are you ready to love the life you have while you create the most extraordinary life you can imagine? Are you ready to take the lead in your family and achieve your vision of ideal family life? Are you ready to develop deep and satisfying relationships with your children and become the amazing parent you always wanted to be? Are you ready to dream of castles and take action to build them? Are you ready to not only master your own personal growth and self-leadership, but to lead others to win their battles? Are you ready to defeat your demons, addictions and distractions by gaining and sustaining daily disciplines?

Good! Keep reading, because this book gives you exactly what you need to do it!

Hal Elrod
Author of *The Miracle Morning* which
has sold over 2 million copies.

*Embrace your body,
home and business.*

PREFACE

BUILD YOUR DREAM CASTLE

Embrace your body, home and business

In my work as a speaker, coach and consultant, I am often asked how to achieve steady success. Today many people are seeking guidance on advancing towards their goals, looking for practical steps to turn their ambitions into reality.

This book encapsulates my extensive experience in guiding entrepreneurs through the Castle System, a comprehensive framework that, while initially tailored for entrepreneurs, offers valuable insights applicable to anyone in pursuit of progression. It leverages the powerful metaphor of a castle–complete with a drawbridge, moat, and five foundational towers: Vision, Beliefs, Habits, Environment, and Discipline–to illustrate the universal principles of achieving success and personal growth.

The castle symbolizes ***our three most important possessions:*** 1) body/life, 2) home/family, and 3) business/profession. If properly constructed and maintained, your castle will support your physical, spiritual, mental, emotional, social and financial health.

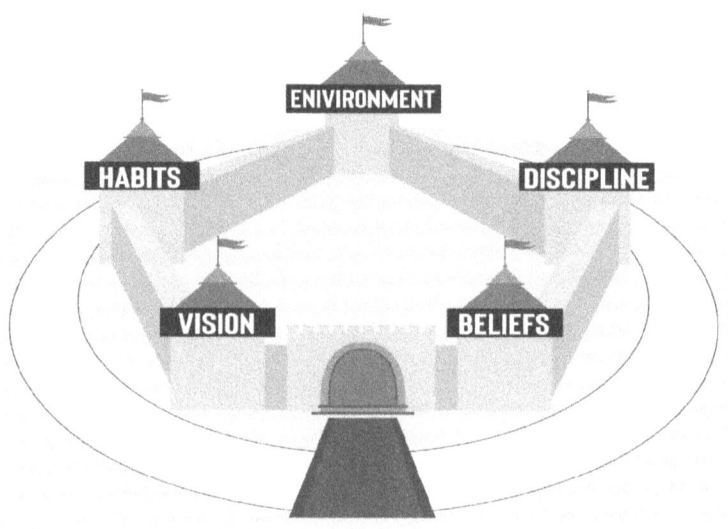

Your Body/Life Castle

The human body–and by extension, a person's life–has often been compared to a castle, temple, or sanctuary. As the Bible says, *"Do you not know that your bodies are temples of the Holy Spirit, who is in you, whom you have received from God? You are not your own; you were bought at a price. Therefore, honor God with your bodies."* (Corinthians 6:19-20)

In Buddhism you find the concept of the Vastu Purusha Mandela, which unifies the proportions of the human body with every form of physical architecture. This symbolically–and to many Buddhists, literally–unites the human body with its larger, more durable outer shell. Your castle/body helps you perform your daily duties and signifies your values and life attainment to others.

People once wore their wealth on their bodies. In museums we see paintings of noblemen and princesses whose rich garments are covered with jewels and pearls. When such people entered a room, everyone knew their social status by their clothing.

Peasants wore peasant garb. Church officials wore church raiment. Criminals were branded to show others their conviction. People with physical deformities or disfiguring diseases like leprosy were shunned. Outward beauty was celebrated. In essence, your physical appearance was seen to be a literal manifestation of the condition of your soul.

Your personal castle–your body–is partly your creation and partly the creation of your ancestors. Your castle will reflect your ancestry for as long as you live, but much of your castle is your responsibility. You can build it higher and stronger, or let it fall into ruin.

Today your physical body may be in disrepair after years of deferred maintenance, neglect, or deterioration from inner and outer demons as you focused on other goals. The good news is you can improve your fitness. If you cannot get out of bed, you can strengthen your arms. If you can only walk across the room, you can learn to walk down the hall. If you can run around the block, you can run a mile. If you can do one push-up, you can condition yourself to do ten or more.

Your Home/Family Castle

Your home provides shelter from the elements. The exterior is often designed to have curb appeal. Likewise, the interior of your home castle might be lavishly furnished.

Your home is a social and family gathering place–a place where you raise children if you choose, and a place where you celebrate happy times and mourn sad events. Your home castle may provide living space for multiple generations of your family and a home for your pets. It holds and protects treasured family heirlooms. If you work from home, it may also be your economic center.

Like your body, your home castle has the dual responsibilities of keeping *in* the good things and keeping *out* the bad things–of keeping in happy memories and keeping out menacing threats!

Your Business/Profession Castle

Your business is also your castle, as it supplies the income you need to live comfortably. Like your body and home, it also requires care and maintenance. And as with your body and home, transformation is triggered by overcoming distractions and focusing on what truly matters.

If your body, home, or business castle is in disrepair, you can rebuild it by taking the necessary remedial actions and making them consistent habits. You can do this at any age–twenty, forty, or eighty. Sustainability results from consistent performance and meticulous maintenance.

Principle of Proactivity: Taking Action on Priorities

The Castle System is based on the ***principle of proactivity***–taking actions, often preventive or preemptive actions–aligned with priorities, vision, and values, and aimed at creating a sustainable winning streak. For example: I keep my five priorities in the center of my castle.

With a powerful castle strategy, balance, progress, and success are within your reach whenever you are willing to take the first step–even when your reach seemingly exceeds your grasp.

> *A man's reach should exceed his grasp,*
> *or what's a heaven for?*
>
> *– Robert Browning*

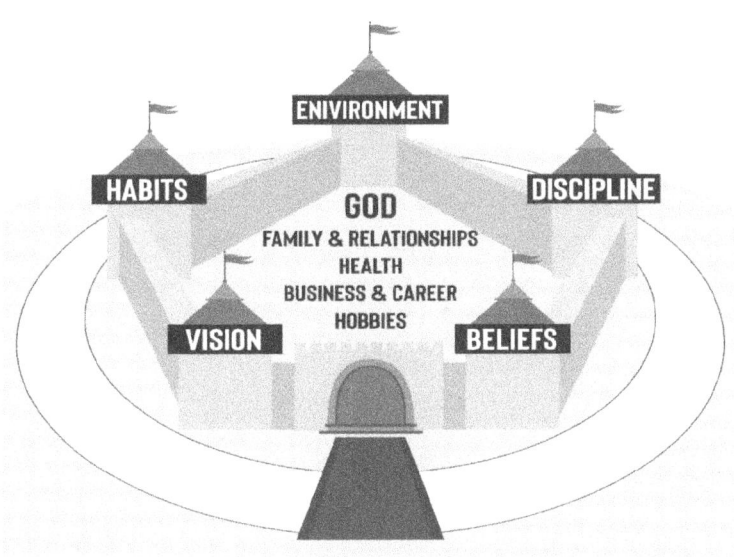

A Lesson in Coping with Setbacks I believe in the truism: ***What is most personal is most universal***. And so, in this preface, I share a painful personal story with the hope that it will help you cope with your challenges and overcome your setbacks.

In spring 1997, I was sixteen and living in Utah. My parents ran an embroidery business, often making long, ten-hour drives from Utah to California to deliver orders in a large white cargo van.

One weekend my dad returned home from California only to pick up my brothers, my sister, and me, and turn around and do it again. We went along because we had a tennis tournament to play in California. As you can imagine, Dad was exhausted but we were anxious to get on the road. And so we piled in the van and my dad got back behind the wheel to drive.

The van was filled to the brim with us kids and with boxes of another shipment of embroidery. My mom stayed home to manage the day-to-day business. I remember my mom standing in the driveway waving goodbye as we pulled away. My two younger brothers Danny and Mike, along with my sister Tiff and I, made ourselves as comfortable as possible lying on sleeping bags between boxes. None of us wore seatbelts.

Just past the midpoint of the journey, near Las Vegas, my dad turned to me. He asked me to take a turn driving to let him catch a few moments of sleep. I was young, self-centered, and more worried about my performance at the upcoming tournament than my dad's fatigue. I told him I wouldn't drive because I needed to rest for the tournament.

Danny, my ten-year-old brother, volunteered to sit in the front to keep my dad company. But shortly thereafter Danny, just like the rest of us kids, drifted off to sleep. My dad continued to drive, fighting exhaustion and trying to make it to the next rest stop. Unfortunately, he missed the rest stop and had another thirty-mile drive until the next one.

Tragically, we never made it to the next rest stop.

Fatigue overtook my dad. The van drifted onto the rumble strips at the highway's edge. The jarring noise startled him awake, he overcorrected the steering, and the van tipped over and started rolling. The police later said it rolled eleven times!

Facing Grief and Guilt

I was awakened by the sound of my own heartbeat pounding in my ears, intertwined with the terrible echo of the rumble strips. In the terrifying seconds that followed, so much happened so fast. Even today, the memories of rolling in the van are hard to decipher. I can't remember how it all happened, but I vividly remember when the van finally stopped rolling and came to a stop.

It was eerily quiet. Panic kicked in instantly as I worried that my family was dead. I was desperate to hear their voices. We each called out to confirm our safety. Dad–good. Mike–okay. Tiff–scared but okay. Me–alive. Danny–silence.

We called again for Danny. Nothing.

Dad kicked out the windshield, climbed through the jagged opening, and ran around yelling for Danny. Dad found him lying in the middle of the road, on his back, looking upward. He was lifeless.

I couldn't comprehend that sight at the time. It was too much for me to handle. I was in shock. My baby brother was gone. How was this real?

An RV stopped to help us. We climbed in. As we sat inside in shock, my dad couldn't hold back his guilt and sorrow. He repeatedly sobbed, "I killed Danny."

A heavy wave of guilt washed over me. I should have driven. I knew how tired my dad was. I knew he had been driving all day. I was utterly selfish and worried only about the tennis tournament.

My guilt was made worse by the overwhelming grief of losing my brother. I thought, "Danny would still be here if I had taken the wheel." As I sat in that RV, listening to my dad's pain and trying to process my own, I told myself that nothing would be normal ever again.

Finding Purpose in Tragedy

That was the worst day of my life. But neighbors and friends surrounded my family and we all cared for each other. I remember my parents telling us kids that "trials make or break us." They helped me process my pain and look for any positives to strengthen our relationship with God. They told me that life was precious and that Danny would want me to live to the fullest. There was much heartache and guilt to work through for me and for my dad, especially.

I asked myself, "What can I do to feel better? What can I do to help my family heal?" My brother Danny would never live the moments that I could live. He would never have a first kiss, or make a high school sports team, or fall in love.

> *"Death leaves a heartache no one can heal;*
> *love leaves a memory no one can steal."*
>
> *– Irish Proverb*

As I reflected on Danny's death, I realized that I didn't want to spend my life wallowing in sorrow and guilt. Instead of succumbing to self-pity, I wanted to live a life big enough for both Danny and me. Despite the grief–or perhaps spurred by it–I became determined to create the most meaningful memories I could from my experiences, which I could then share with the ones I love and not miss a moment to live my best life. I wanted to have the experiences he would never have, in a way that would make him proud; but I also wanted to do that for myself.

I Find a Meaningful Motto

In the aftermath of this terrible time in my life, I found a new motto:

> *"Die with memories, not just dreams."*

To be clear, I didn't have those exact words at that time. It wasn't until seventeen years later that I came across the phrase, and it hit me that this adage was something I had intuitively known and lived by since the accident. I made it my motto because it summed up everything for me and still guides my actions.

Losing Danny was one of the biggest hardships in my life and my family's lives as well. But it was also the beginning of learning how to create my life on purpose and how to follow a powerful strategy to make it happen.

For me, Danny's tragic death was a ***turning point***. Most people experience some tragedy in their life–an accident or setback that changes the trajectory of their life. I often wonder what would have happened if I had focused solely on my guilt, depression, and loss after Danny died. I don't know, but I can tell you I *would not* be where I am today. I am grateful that Danny's death, as tragic as it was, helped me mold myself at a young age.

I hope that you won't need a terrible personal loss to awaken in you the desire and drive to ***make wonderful memories*** that last a lifetime. I encourage you to dream and to set ambitious goals, and to believe that that even the biggest goals can be achieved one small step at a time. Every small victory brings you one step closer to the health, wealth, and happiness you deserve!

We know life does not last forever and that we all have to die someday. But this fact should not discourage us; rather, it should inspire us to live fully in the precious time we have.

When my brother Danny died, I learned that life on earth can be short. Having that perspective at an early age changed my life for the better. I felt that I had to dream big and act bigger. We all have twenty-four hours in a day, and it's how we spend our time that defines us. I now live my motto: ***Die with memories, not just dreams***. The most important thing you and I can do in our lives is to create meaningful moments and memories that last a lifetime.

DIE WITH MEMORIES NOT JUST DREAMS

INTRODUCTION

NAVIGATING GROWTH: STRATEGIES FOR PERSONAL AND PROFESSIONAL ADVANCEMENT

In writing this book, I have one clear aim: to facilitate your gain, your growth, and your development. In fact, **the very structure of this book serves as a sequential personal and professional development model.** I have designed this book to be more than a just good read.

I invite you to take seven actions: Vision, Belief, Priorities, Action, Win Streaks, Environment, and Discipline.

Take these seven actions in three degrees of intensity or duration: Minimum, Medium, and Maximum.My intent is to give you a clear path forward and provide support for the rigorous ascent. To make the lessons and insights more memorable, I have added several inspiring stories of people who have conquered their demons and left behind rich memories and legacies for themselves and for others to enjoy.

Three Sections and Seven Actions

When making a movie, the director will set up the scene and then call for "action." That is the standard cue for all actors to start their performance and for the crew to begin filming.

In a sense I am serving temporarily in the role of director, assisting you in making the movie of your ideal life. And, like any director, I carefully set the scene and call for you to take action – seven sequential actions that will take you from where you are today to where you want to go.

Section 1 introduces ***three actions*** to help you clarify who you are, what you want, and what matters most to you:

- Action 1: Craft a Clear Vision.
- Action 2: Believe in the Inevitability of Your Success.
- Action 3: Pick Your Top Priorities.

Once you see clearly who you are and what you want, believe in the inevitability of your success, and select your top priorities, you have a firm foundation for your dream castle.

Section 2 introduces ***three more actions*** that build momentum:

- Action 4: Master the Minimum Actions.
- Action 5: Create and Celebrate Win Streaks.
- Action 6: Create a Supportive Environment.

Once you are taking constructive actions in the desired direction, creating tremendous momentum by Mastering the Minimums and celebrating win streaks in a supportive environment, you are well on your way to building your ideal dream castles.

Section 3 introduces the one action that sustains success:

- Action 7: Defeat Demons/Distractions with Discipline.

Please see and say this simple truth: "If it's going to be, it's up to me.""

> *"There's a lot of blood, sweat, and guts between dreams and success."*
>
> *– Bear Bryant*

Yes, it's your time and your life. You can envision and enjoy your dream castles, starting today, by taking these seven powerful actions. These actions constitute a development system.

> *"You do not rise to the level of your goals. You fall to the level of your systems."*
>
> *James Clear*

DIE WITH MEMORIES NOT JUST DREAMS

SECTION 1

CLARIFY WHAT YOU WANT

In Section 1 you are invited to take the first three actions:

Action 1: Craft a Clear Vision

Action 2: Believe in the Inevitability of Your Success

Action 3: Pick Your Top Priorities

Action 1: Craft a Clear Vision

Living fully begins with dreams. It's good to have dreams about what we want to achieve in life. We all need a vision of how our lives could be better, for ourselves and for our loved ones.

> *Hold fast to dreams*
> *For if dreams die*
> *Life is a broken-winged bird*
> *That cannot fly.*
>
> *Hold fast to dreams*
> *For when dreams go*
> *Life is a barren field*
> *Frozen with snow.*
>
> *— Dreams by Langston Hughes*

If you hope to die at a ripe old age with plenty of happy memories, not with unfulfilled dreams, you need to take a leap of faith and create your future.

> *"The future is not some place we are going to, but one we are creating. The paths are not to be found but made. And the activity of making them changes both the maker and the destination."*
>
> *— John Schaar*

When I started my entrepreneurial journey, I had big plans for my life. Dreaming big has always come naturally to me.

During my college years, my primary focus was tennis. While attending classes, I struggled to focus on the professors. Instead of listening to the teacher, I would be daydreaming and jotting down ideas in my notebook. Its pages were filled with concepts and possibilities. Whenever an idea would pop into my head, I would think about how it aligned with the future I wanted to have. I wanted to be a present husband and father, committed to quality moments with my children, coaching their sports teams, and supporting them through life's crucial junctures because it is all about dying with memories, not dreams.

I invite you to think of a time when you took ***a leap of faith***–the sensation of uncertainty mingled with excitement, the whispering doubts, and the roaring determination. These narratives are not unique to celebrities or extraordinary individuals. They reside within each of us. Every struggle we face, every challenge we overcome, is a chapter in the grand novel of our lives. And like any gripping story, ours is filled with ups and downs, trials and tribulations, joy and sorrow.

What is your dream? Do you envision yourself persevering against all odds, seeing your dreams come true and becoming the best version of yourself?

> *"If you want to be happy, set an aspiration that commands your thoughts, liberates your energy, and inspires your hope."*
>
> *– Andrew Carnegie*

Remember: Your vision doesn't have to be carved in stone. But it does need to stretch you and give you a purpose beyond just "making it through the day." Your vision becomes the compass by which you navigate life's ups and downs.

Your long-term vision enables you to keep your daily struggles in perspective. When you create a life with clear intent, you can live out your vision! I assure you: God didn't send you to this earth to be average!

Vision: A Blueprint for Building Your Castle

During the early stages of my business, I lacked clear vision. But I persisted in clarifying and documenting my vision. Over time, my vision sharpened, and the "how" gradually revealed itself.

Indeed, "when your vision is sufficiently vast, the means to realize it will manifest." I can personally attest to this. As my vision became clearer the necessary actions unfolded before me.

Admittedly, the journey is rarely smooth; but I refuse to surrender my dreams. Settling for anything less than the vision I aspired to achieve is unacceptable. My focus centers on Mastering the Minimum actions aligned with my vision for a fulfilling life. I reject the notion of merely building wealth at the cost of quality time with my family. I found a way to build wealth and be with my family, leveraging my time and generating the desired income.

If you harbor lofty dreams and aspirations, I encourage you to keep dreaming. After high school, too few of us have big dreams. If we do, they quickly leave. Whether that's because of the fear of judgment, the fear of failure, or whatever you fear, it's time to think bigger.

I invite you to envision and enact a life of purpose and meaning, shaped by your heart's desires, and craft ***a compelling vision or mission statement for your future.*** This statement establishes unwavering priorities in alignment with your aspirations, cultivates a nurturing environment, and deploys intentional actions to manifest your dreams.

As you live these principles, you translate your knowledge into action every day to bring your dreams to fruition. Be prepared to focus on your aspirations, devote yourself fully, invest the requisite time and effort, and persevere through storms with unwavering discipline. As you commit wholeheartedly to these principles and apply them to your life, you will construct a life that surpasses your wildest dreams and become the person you were always meant to be.

Serena Williams: Foggy Vision, Then a Blitz!

In 2011, **Serena Williams** stood at a crossroads in her illustrious tennis career. Despite winning thirteen Grand Slam titles, she grappled with a profound sense of uncertainty and self-doubt. This wasn't just a minor setback, but a soul-crushing dilemma that threatened to eclipse her once-glorious reign in tennis.

She had suffered unexpected losses in pivotal matches, including defeats in Grand Slam tournaments that were once her domain. These losses shook her confidence. Injuries began to plague her, disrupting her training routines and casting shadows of doubt.

The turmoil within her was palpable. Critics and pundits questioned whether Serena's era of dominance was ending. Her performances on the court were marked by wavering focus and lapses in form. It was a challenging period that tested her mental and physical resilience.

Enter **Patrick Mouratoglou**, the coach who would become Serena's guiding light through the fog of uncertainty. Together, they embarked on a meticulous journey of self-discovery and improvement. They pored over countless game films, dissecting her weaknesses and crafting strategic plans for the battles ahead.

Mouratoglou's mentorship wasn't just about refining her tennis skills and instilling a renewed sense of purpose and unshakable confidence.

Their collaboration was about making tactical game plans and constructing a legacy that would withstand the test of time. This was a true blitz effort to strengthen her game.

Serena's transformation was nothing short of remarkable. The post-2011 chapter of Serena's career showed her commitment to her determination. She secured an additional ten Grand Slam titles, solidifying her status as one of the greatest tennis players in history.

Her accomplishments extended beyond numbers and statistics. Serena shattered records for the most Grand Slam singles titles, including the Women's Open Era. She became the oldest woman to win a Grand Slam and reclaimed her World No. 1 ranking multiple times.

Lessons for us: Serena Williams emerged from the fog of uncertainty not just as a champion, but as an inspiration to countless aspiring athletes and individuals in all walks of life. Her journey teaches us that sometimes the most formidable battles are the ones fought within ourselves with our inner demons. Serena's story reminds us that with resilience, the proper guidance, and unwavering self-belief, we can mount a Blitz and triumph over adversity and achieve greatness.

Often we lack clarity in what we want and where we are headed and forget why we set our vision in the first place. I call this *foggy vision*. It's the fog that settles in just when we are starting to take action in our lives. It's the fog of doubt about what we are building. When we set visions without a clear purpose, it becomes easy to veer off track when faced with challenges because we forget *why*.

Foggy vision arises when we lack belief in our ability to achieve our aspirations. We often set lofty visions without genuinely believing that we can attain them. We start taking action, but when things get tough we give up and tell ourselves, "I knew I couldn't do it," or "It was foolish to think I could accomplish this." We lack belief in our vision.

Our Inevitable First Fight

When my wife Janei'a and I were dating, we had our first fight. Afterward, I feared that we would break up. I wasn't worried about my personal feelings for her. I knew I wanted to be with her. I was worried *she* would have second thoughts about a long-term relationship with *me*. I loved her, but my vision became foggy as I questioned her intentions. Demons of uncertainty clouded my understanding of our future together and I started to doubt and question everything.

After the argument had passed, I asked her, "So what does this mean for us going forward?"

She looked at me and calmly responded, "We will have many fights and disagreements. This was just our first one. It is normal and part of being in a committed relationship."

Janei'a possessed a clear long-term vision for our relationship. She understood our commitment and recognized that disagreements were part of the journey. I am incredibly fortunate to have her in my life. Her words made the fog surrounding me disappear. I realized that our relationship's success meant embracing positive and challenging conversations.

Commitment to your vision plays a vital role in determining success. In our marriage, we have had our fair share of disagreements–small ones every few days and significant ones every few months. Both of us possess strong personalities. However, we remain committed. When we married, we made a pact never to utter the word "divorce." Throughout our marriage, we have never uttered the word, even though there have been times when she probably contemplated it during my less-than-stellar moments.

Clear Vision Keeps You Focused

Your commitment and clarity of vision enable you to stay focused on what you aim to create. When your vision lacks clarity, revisit your vision and mission. Why did you set this vision in the first place? Feeling uncertain about your vision and aspirations for the future is expected. Remember that gaining clarity is a gradual process that requires time and intention.

Foggy vision can divert your focus, making it easier for others to attack your castle. It is much easier for others to challenge your vision when you question it yourself!

Imagine a life just living day to day, with no vision of the future. You get up in the morning, go to work, eat some food, go home, go to sleep, and do it all over again the next day. You have no goals for the future and so your castle remains unchanged.

Maybe you do the Minimum to maintain it, but you make no major improvements. Then, after eighty or ninety years, you die. Your life is soon forgotten because you did nothing notable, memorable, or interesting.

Sounds dreary, doesn't it? Sadly, it accurately describes the life of far too many people.

You and I are born with the desire to create a vision of the future and with the drive to improve that future by taking action daily. We can say, "My castle is insufficient. I want to make it bigger and more beautiful. I'll begin planning the renovation today and expect to be done in one year."

Vision shouldn't be a pipe dream, but a practical tool guiding your daily actions. In your mind's eye you see what you want–a more beautiful castle, a better job, a happy family, a respected position in your community–and you *take action* to make it happen.

Imagine seeing your life's vision through a pair of ***magic glasses***. They would show you possibilities, opportunities, and the future. They would guide you toward your desired income and outcome, showing a blueprint of your future. If such glasses were available in a store, you would rush to get them! How much would you pay for them? How often would you wear them? You would likely stand in line for hours to have your own pair of "***magic vision glasses***."

Luckily, you and I don't need to wait; we can craft a clear vision now to see the path ahead and to focus on our ultimate goal.

Power of Clear Vision

When we get absorbed in immediate and urgent tasks, we tend to lose sight of our larger goals. When this happens we feel like we're in a rut, just going through the motions with no purpose or direction. And the only race we run is the proverbial rat race.

The antidote to this feeling of listless ennui is creating a clear vision for your life. Vision is a transformative force, a compass that provides direction in the vast sea of life's uncertainties. Your vision provides orientation for your actions. A clear vision can pull you forward out of ruts and routines towards your end-in-mind goal.

The key is to keep updating your vision as you evolve and progress. Often, as adults, we have realized our initial vision for our lives. We may start to think we're too old or too tired to create something extraordinary. At any age, when we stop having a proactive vision for our future we tend to become reactive victims. We become resigned to the fact that our life is what it is and we can't do anything about it.

As we age, mature and change, we can continue to revise and refine the vision. You may have reached certain milestones–graduation, marriage, a dream job–and wondered, "What's next?" Creating a fresh vision is like opening a new chapter in your favorite book. It's exciting, full of possibilities, and tailored to what you need and want now.

Would you ever embark on a trip without knowing the destination? Certainly not! Imagine yourself as a ship captain. Without a vision or a destination, your ship would drift aimlessly in the vast ocean. But with a clear destination in mind, you can navigate through challenges and make course corrections as needed to reach your desired harbor.

If your castle has no running water, then your vision might be to install indoor plumbing! If no one in your family has more than a high school diploma, your vision might be to be the first to graduate from college. Your vision might be to get married and have children, or it might be to start your own company. It's totally up to you! No one can create your vision but you.

Vision Turns Challenges into Triumphs

Vision molds our choices at every juncture, from the jobs we take to the relationships we nurture. Vision is the starting point for achieving everything you want, from being an excellent parent to starting a business. Every decision, big or small, is influenced by your overarching vision. But remember: Having a vision doesn't guarantee immediate success. Failure and setbacks are part and parcel of life.

> *"You need to be stubborn on your vision, but very flexible on the details."*
>
> *– Jeff Bezos*

What distinguishes those who succeed is the vision they hold on to during trying times. Perhaps you've faced a business failure or a personal setback. Reflect on how a robust and resilient vision could have, or did, help you navigate through those choppy waters.

Vision is more than just a lofty goal or dream; it's a guiding light, an anchor in the stormy seas of life. It's never too late to clarify your vision and align your actions with it. It's the difference between aimlessly wandering and purposefully journeying. And in the end, it's not just about reaching the destination but about who you become along the way.

Mindy Kaling: Creating Her Own Vision

Mindy Kaling: Triumph Over Hollywood's Stereotypes

In the early 2000s, Mindy Kaling faced a defining moment that tested her resolve like never before. Despite her undeniable talent, she was often typecast or overlooked due to her ethnicity and appearance. One particular instance that stands out occurred shortly after her graduation from Dartmouth College when she auditioned for a role in a popular TV comedy. Instead of being judged on her performance, she was told, quite bluntly, that she wasn't the "right fit" for television. The implication was clear: Hollywood's narrow definitions of beauty and talent did not accommodate a young Indian-American woman with aspirations of being both in front of the camera and behind it.

Refusing to be deterred by this disheartening experience, Kaling channeled her frustration into motivation. She co-wrote and starred in a play titled *Matt & Ben*, a comedy about Matt Damon and Ben Affleck that quickly became a surprise hit in the New York theater scene. This success catapulted her into the spotlight, leading to her breakthrough as a writer and actress on *The Office* at the age of twenty-four. Her role on *The Office* wasn't handed to her; she earned it through relentless perseverance and a showcase of her multifaceted talent.

The real turning point came with *The Mindy Project*, where she leveraged her position to challenge and change the industry's standards. Against significant odds, she ensured the show featured a diverse cast and crew, addressing the very biases that once threatened to hold her back. Her efforts paid off spectacularly: *The Mindy Project* became a beacon of progress in Hollywood, with Mindy Kaling leading the charge as one of the first women of color to create, write, and star in her own show. Under her leadership, the show not only entertained millions but also pushed forward the conversation about diversity in Hollywood, paving the way for future generations.

Resolution and Legacy:

Mindy Kaling's journey from a young playwright facing rejection to a celebrated creator and actress is a powerful testament to her resilience. Her achievements include multiple awards and nominations, bestselling books, and influential roles in major film projects. Beyond her personal accolades, Kaling's greatest accomplishment may be her role in shifting Hollywood's landscape towards a more inclusive and diverse industry.

Personal Development Insights:

Mindy Kaling's story is a compelling reminder that the path to achieving one's vision often includes navigating through prejudice and adversity. Her determination to transform her trials into triumphs not only carved out a space for her in Hollywood but also laid the groundwork for others to follow. It challenges us to ask ourselves: faced with rejection and stereotypes, how can we persist and create our own opportunities for success?

So, ask yourself, "If I had vision glasses, what would I want to see? And how might I make my vision a reality?"

Pure vs. False Desires

In our journey towards our respective visions, we need to differentiate between **_pure desires,_** those that guide us towards our true purpose and life mission, and **_false desires_**, those that are deceptive lures sidetracking our quest for happiness.

Pure desires are the deep-seated aspirations that motivate us to evolve into our finest selves, fueling our drive for personal growth and deeper connections.

In contrast, false desires are fleeting temptations that offer temporary satisfaction but ultimately leading us astray.

Embracing our pure desires is about aligning with our innermost ambitions and fostering a more profound connection with what's most important to us.

The ancient Greeks recognized different types of happiness:

The first is _hedonistic_ happiness or temporary pleasure. It relates to sensory enjoyment and is transitory.

Eudaimonic happiness comes from finding purpose and meaning in life. _Eudaimonic_ happiness is long-lasting and produces moral satisfaction, personal fulfillment and growth.

Your vision for your future should be guided by pure desires, eudaimonic fulfillment, and the building of meaningful memories.

Clarity and Specificity of Vision

Why does the clarity and specificity of your vision matter so much? You cannot take progressive steps towards fulfilling your vision if you aren't sure exactly what it is!

In 2006, I was a poor young student and recently married. I wanted success but was uncertain about what success meant to me and how to achieve it. Lon Wardrop, a friend and mentor, challenged me to get specific about my vision.

Initially, my vision was vague. I wanted to be financially secure and a good husband and father. When I told Lon my goals, he told me that I would never attain success because my vision was fuzzy. He said, "Vague visions get muddy results. You need to be specific about what you want in your life."

As I got more specific, my vision became clear and it felt more achievable.

My initial vague goal of owning a house morphed into a clear vision of owning a spacious home complete with a game room, theater room, pool, and tennis court. I visualized my children having their friends over for fun and games. Although these aspirations seemed monumental then, the specifics clarified my vision and allowed me to create a step-by-step plan to actualize it.

Years later, we moved into that dream house–our castle! My wife and I enjoy a busy household of kids and their friends. It's a hub of activity, a home that embodies the vision my wife and I had.

It's incredible to look back and realize that these were the dreams I was too afraid to voice, thinking they were too grand or unrealistic. But once I understood what I wanted and why, the actions started to make sense. Eventually, everything started to fall into place.

Create a Vision Bigger Than Your Worst Day

You may receive such a dire problem or prognosis that it dooms any dreams or ambitions. Every day can become a struggle against the physical limitations that seek to confine your mind and body. Your life becomes a race against time, the relentless pursuit of a vision, driven by an unwavering resolve that pushes you to greater heights even as your physical abilities dwindle.

You and I may die with some unfulfilled dreams, but we can still have many wonderful memories. Our castles can still stand bright and shining, high on a hill. Your life can become an inspiring story of overcoming adversity, an instructive example of the power of having a clear vision that enables you to persevere and prosper.

Clear vision fuels innovation, creativity, and success. Often it's not the absence of motivation that hampers progress, but the lack of a clear vision. Your vision has to be resilient enough to weather the storm of a bad day when your mood swings like a pendulum.

We all have bad days. The question is this: who are you on those days? Do you abandon workouts, lose your temper, or let frustration rule? This is where ***the power of vision*** comes into play.

When your vision is to be the best dad or mom, you may still yell at your kids on a tough day. But you are quick to recognize it, apologize, and realign with your core values.

When did you last get crystal clear on your vision? Imagine if your best friend asked you, "What's your vision for your life right now?" Would you have an answer ready, or are you just coasting through life? Do you genuinely know what you want in vivid detail?

Remember the adage: "If you don't know what you want, you end up with a lot you don't want."

Don't Be Your Own Worst Enemy!

Crafting a clear vision is crucial to creating the life you want. Keep an open mind, be creative, and don't hesitate to revise your vision as you learn more about yourself and your desires.

And, don't talk yourself out of wanting and desiring good things.

When I coach clients on their vision, they'll come up with a big vision statement for their life: "I want to buy a motorhome and travel for six months out of the year with our family."

Two days later, they might message me back. "Maybe that vision is too big. I decided to change it to renting an RV twice a year for a long weekend to take our kids to the local lake."

They talked themselves out of their big vision! Don't let this happen to you. Allow yourself to believe that anything is possible in your life. You don't need to tell anyone else about it or know how you will make it happen right now. Just allow yourself to have a vision for the life you want to create.

And be as specific as you can about your vision. Use pictures, sounds, smells, words–whatever you need to create the vision you want for your life. Understand that your vision is yours alone. You can make it whatever you want.

Mr. Beast: Channeling Vision into Relentless Pursuit

In the noise of YouTube, **Mr. Beast**–known to his friends and family as *Jimmy Donaldson* from Greenville, North Carolina–found himself at a critical juncture. His channel was stuck on a plateau of 8,000 subscribers, even though he had poured his heart into every video.

His journey began when he stumbled upon an ambitious, almost impossible idea: donating thousands of dollars to unsuspecting strangers.

Mr. Beast's vision wasn't just about creating content and hoping for the best. In 2015, when he was in high school and had about 8,000 subscribers, he made a bold move. In a dimly lit room, using a low-quality camera, Mr. Beast declared in a video titled "Hi: me in 5 years" that he would have over one million followers. He was only eighteen, yet he spoke with the conviction of a future Internet sensation.

This was no mere whim. It was a gamble. A tremendous risk. He invested every dollar he had into these random acts of kindness, broadcasting them on his channel, when the payoff was far from guaranteed.

Critics lambasted him and doubted his motives, and even his closest friends questioned his sanity. The endeavor drained his finances, but something more substantial was at stake: his reputation, his integrity, and the essence of who he was as a creator.

The tension escalated to its peak when a particular donation almost backfired, leaving him with legal troubles and mounting debts. He was on the brink, teetering at the edge of a precipice that could swallow his dreams whole.

But Mr. Beast refused to succumb. To make his vision a reality, he fought back with grit, determination, and an unshakable belief, turning the tide in his favor. He built relationships with sponsors, orchestrated collaborations with other creators, and continued his philanthropic adventures with renewed vigor.

The resolution unfolded like a masterpiece. The controversial decision to donate paid off as his channel exploded. Within a year he had reached a staggering one million subscribers, and the numbers kept soaring. His videos became a phenomenon, attracting billions of views and earning millions in revenue.

His biggest challenge was transformed into his most celebrated triumph. His mission to impact lives positively became a global movement, inspiring others to act with generosity and empathy.

In 2022, Donaldson ranked on the *Forbes* list for the highest paid YouTube creator. In 2023, *Time* magazine named him as one of the world's 100 most influential people. With an estimated net worth of $500 million, he employed over 250 people including writers, editors, and producers. On October 15th, 2023, Donaldson surpassed 200 million YouTube subscribers!

Donaldson's journey encapsulates the relentless pursuit of vision, a battle fought with unwavering resolve, and success that stands as a monument to innovation and courage. He had a vision and he built it one video at a time. His unwavering belief in his future resonates with entrepreneurs and visionaries worldwide. He serves as a powerful example to the transformative power of risk taking with an unwavering self-belief, lessons that resonate with dreamers everywhere.

Since Jimmy Donaldson was only twenty-six years old as of 2024, you can bet that many decades from now he'll die with many amazing memories!

Lessons for us: When we read a story about a winner like Donaldson, we tend to feel inspired momentarily and then move on. However, the true magic lies in being inspired and ***acting on that inspiration.***

As you define your vision, remember that clarity is key. Your vision should be detailed and actionable, and should resonate with your deepest aspirations. Aim for a vision that gets you out of bed in the morning, motivates you to strive valiantly, and encourages you to take risks and learn from failures.

Don't allow scarcity to limit your vision! Allow yourself to believe that you can make this happen. Believe that you are made for more and that when you take your life seriously by getting clear about what you want and taking action, God, the universe, and whatever you believe in will help you along the way.

Chief Regret of the Dying: Sacrificing Family

Dr. Bronnie Ware, an Australian nurse who spent several years working in palliative care, provided care to patients in the last weeks of their lives. Through her experiences, she compiled insights from conversations with over two hundred patients, primarily aged between sixty and ninety years old. These individuals, reflecting on their lives, shared their regrets and the wisdom they had gained with Ware, hoping others might learn from their experiences.

One of the most poignant and recurring themes Ware observed was the regret of having spent too much time on work and not enough with family. This regret was not limited to a few; it was a sentiment echoed by a significant majority of her patients. They spoke of long hours dedicated to their careers at the expense of meaningful interactions and experiences with their loved ones.

Patients recounted missed family dinners, unattended birthday parties, and absence from milestone family events like graduations and weddings. They spoke of the realization, too late, that the pursuit of professional success had come at a steep personal cost. Ware noted that these reflections often came with a sense of sorrow for time that could not be reclaimed and relationships that could have been deeper.

In response to these reflections, Ware was inspired to share these lessons more broadly, emphasizing the importance of finding a balance between work and personal life. She highlighted the critical need to prioritize relationships and moments that bring joy and fulfillment beyond professional achievements.

The insights gathered by Ware from her conversations with patients serve as a powerful reminder of the finite nature of time and the importance of prioritizing what truly matters. Her work encourages a reevaluation of how we balance our commitments and urges us to make conscious choices about how we spend our time, with an emphasis on nurturing the relationships that enrich our lives.

> *"No other success can compensate for failure in the home."*
>
> *– David O. McKay*

While your work is important and essential, it should not eclipse nurturing close familial relationships. It's about striking a balance where professional commitments and personal connections coexist, enriching our lives with a blend of achievement and affection. Remember, the memories we create with those we care about often become our most treasured legacy.

Our Vision: Family and Friends

My wife Janei'a and I started our marriage with a family vision. We now have four incredibly unique kids: Cade, nineteen years old in 2024; Kaia, seventeen; Kiri, fourteen; and Ren, ten. With them we share some unique family traditions.

First We Turn Milestones into Memories: Family Trip Tradition

Years ago, when Janei'a and I had two young kids, we set a long-term goal: to take our kids, their spouses, and our grandkids on an all-expenses-paid trip. This goal gave both of us a meaningful purpose.

We set this goal when we were so poor that our splurge was eating out once a week at Little Caesar's pizza for $5. This vision still drives what I do every day. I imagine taking our family to fun places and creating memories with them.

Our travels have taken us to many places, including Bora Bora, Cape Town, Dubai, Seychelles, Italy, France, Monaco, Hawaii, Mexico, Belize, and The Maldives, involving both family trips and quiet getaways with my wife.

The essence of these memories isn't rooted in the destinations or in the money spent. Long before financial success, I crafted precious memories without the backdrop of exotic locations. The value of these experiences lies in the moments shared, the conversations, the laughter, and the familial bonds.

As my financial situation evolved, so did the scale of our adventures; but the core joy of creating memories remained constant. Whether it's a simple picnic in the park or exploring a new country, the true wealth lies in the experience and not in the price tag.

At age twelve, each our kids went on a trip with the opposite-gender parent somewhere in the country. Age twelve is a critical time in a child's life–a time when they either connect deeply with you or they start to pull away from you. One-on-one trips with our twelve-year-olds have helped my wife and me create unforgettable memories and close relationships.

When our kids turn sixteen, we take it up a notch. They get to pick any destination in the world to explore with the same-gender parent. Sure, globe-trotting might not be in everyone's budget. But money isn't the point. Creativity is your best currency when it comes to making memories.

I got to go on my first sixteen-year-old trip with our oldest, Cade. We tossed around ideas for an epic journey for months, but nothing clicked. Then we had a light-bulb moment: Dubai and supercars. We combined Cade's car obsession with a place that treats them like royalty. We had found a place that he was excited to visit.

The trip was epic. We went skydiving, explored deserts, cruised in yachts, revved up supercars, and even swam with sharks.

Beyond having Instagram-worthy moments, this one-on-one time was a massive game-changer in our relationship. Today, Cade isn't just my son; he's my wingman and a best friend. I don't think this would have happened if we hadn't experienced those two weeks together.

Janei'a has been on her trips with the kids. So far, she has gone on a twelve-year-old trip with Cade and the big sixteen-year-old trip to Australia with Kaia.

Second: I Coach My Kid's High School Tennis Team

Another dream-turned memory has been ***coaching my kids' high school tennis teams.***

This was a legacy my dad left me–coaching his kids' tennis teams–and it's one I continue. I spend up to twenty-five hours a week for five months each year coaching the team. It's like a part-time job, but I look forward to doing it because I get to have a front-row seat to their lives. I get to experience the highs and lows, their triumphs and defeats.

These shared moments carve out profound impressions. The highs are ecstatic. The lows are a gut punch. But each moment knits us closer together and teaches us about resilience.

I've cheered at game-winning tennis matches and consoled players during disappointing losses. Each instance locks in a memory that no social media could ever capture. Investing twenty-five hours a week for five months a year coaching my kids' high school tennis teams is now part of my legacy, layered with memories that will stand the test of time.

Third: I Conduct Teenage Mastermind Sessions

Two years ago, I desired to create a deeper connection with my children and their circle of friends during their teenage years. I have an amazing network of friends and colleagues. I learn from them all the time, but I was missing chances for my kids to learn from these people.

So, I created ***mastermind sessions*** for my teenagers and their friends. We started with a session titled "Decades in Days" with just five kids. A close friend of mine came to our home and talked to them for two hours about how he had become successful.

I posted a picture of the kids and my buddy on social media, and word spread like wildfire. I had people messaging me from around the country asking if their teens could fly in and attend this mastermind. I couldn't figure out how to make a large event happen, but I decided to invite more local kids. Soon twenty aspiring youths were coming at a ninety percent attendance rate.

These sessions were intense learning experiences packed with actionable advice and insights. The atmosphere was deep focus and engagement; distractions like phones were pushed to the side. Remarkably, after just a few sessions, the kids were so absorbed they didn't even check their phones. They took diligent notes, asked thoughtful questions, and absorbed valuable lessons from seasoned experts in various fields.

My network of friends served as the speakers–each a leader in his or her field. These professionals shared insights they wished someone had shared with them at age sixteen. These weren't just lectures; they were catalysts for change.

When I started this mastermind, I had no idea the impact that it would create in these kids' lives. Over seventeen months, the teenagers launched ventures, excelled in door-to-door sales, and absorbed wisdom from twenty-eight diverse speakers. We made cherished memories. These sessions underscored a profound truth: When you invest in relationships, the return-on-investment (ROI) is immeasurable.

Whether it's a trip to Dubai or a staycation in your backyard, make the investment. Trust me: the returns are incalculable. Yes, you are busy, but make time for the things that matter most–the things that fulfill your vision.

Action 2: Believe in the Inevitability of Your Success

"Belief is the ignition switch that gets you off the launching pad."

– Denis Waitley

"If we did all the things we are capable of, we would literally astound ourselves."

– Thomas Edison

The Example of Thomas Edison

Thomas Edison managed to outpace his contemporaries by believing in the inevitability of his success and persisting. He carried around a pen and paper everywhere he went to ensure he never missed a spark of genius, which became a goldmine of innovation for him.

Still, it took **Thomas Edison** more than ten thousand failed attempts before he successfully created a working light bulb. His vision of creating a revolutionary light source kept him going through countless experiments and many failures. His unwavering vision and resilience eventually led to his groundbreaking invention. His response to his repeated failures was this: "I have not failed ten thousand times– I've successfully found ten thousand ways that will not work."

Edison's ten thousand failed attempts to invent the light bulb serve as a classic example of perseverance and belief. But another story about Edison further cements his legacy as a master of resilience and innovation. After revolutionizing the world with the electric light bulb, Edison embarked on a quest to invent a storage battery to power electric vehicles.

Edison threw himself into this project with his usual zeal. However, he faced a daunting array of technical difficulties. The challenge was creating a safe, reliable, long-lasting battery. Edison experimented with numerous combinations of materials and designs, facing setbacks at every turn. He spent over a decade, from 1900 to 1910, investing much of his fortune into this project.

One striking incident occurred when he thought he had finally cracked the formula. After countless trials, Edison developed a prototype he believed was ready for production. But the batteries started leaking during the initial production phase, rendering them useless. It was a massive blow both financially and emotionally.

Edison refused to give up. He returned undeterred to the drawing board. His persistence paid off when he finally created a nickel-iron battery with big improvements over existing models. While it didn't revolutionize the automobile industry, it found widespread use in industrial applications. For example: For decades, his batteries served as the power source for millions of electric forklifts in warehouses and factories worldwide.

Edison's success was marked by a willingness to confront and overcome seemingly insurmountable challenges. His story in the realm of battery technology vividly illustrates how the step-by-step pursuit of a vision can lead to success, even in the face of repeated failures.

Lessons We Learn from Edison

Here are some lessons that Edison taught us:

Awareness: Be aware of innovative insights and ideas. Every conversation, book, or event can seed an idea worth exploring. Increasing our awareness increases our capacity to spot and capture valuable insights. Always be receptive to innovative ideas; capture them in a notebook or with Voice Memo or the Notes app on a smartphone, and turn them into actions.

Iterative experimentation: Be open to experimentation and testing. Whether trying a new technique in our profession, a new routine in our day or a new approach to an old problem, we believe that each experiment gets us closer to refining our strategy and achieving our goals.

Embracing failure: The road to innovation is riddled with failure. Edison himself said, "I have not failed. I've just found ten thousand ways that won't work." Seeing failures as stepping stones, rather than stumbling blocks, can radically alter our journey towards success.

Standardizing creativity: While creativity is often spontaneous, Edison's method effectively structured it. Carving out dedicated "ideation" or "creative" time in our schedules can yield unexpected and transformative results.

While the tools and times have changed, the principles remain relevant.

Five Stages of Belief

Vision without belief is just daydreaming. Vision needs to be backed by a strong conviction and the willingness to take action to make it a reality. These two powerful forces–vision and belief–can benefit all of us. Vision provides direction, and belief strengthens determination. Without both, even the brightest dreams can fade. But armed with vision and belief, we can turn the seemingly impossible into reality.

When we start taking steps towards our grand vision, we may not start with a firm belief in the inevitability of our success. In fact, we may have serious doubts regarding its possibility or probability. My friend Woody Woodward was the first to explain to me the ***Five Stages of Belief***. I still use this framework with my clients to help them apply vision and belief to their creations.

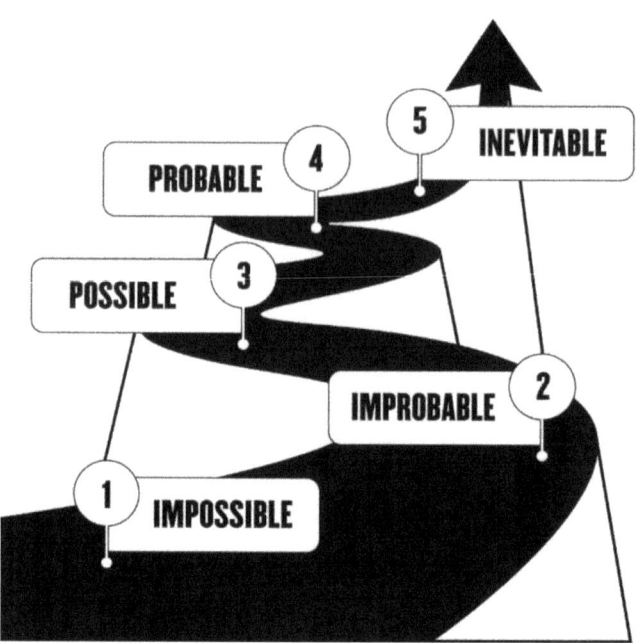

1. ***Impossible.*** At this stage, achieving your goals feels out of reach and possibly results in overwhelming intimidation or discouragement. You need to use your willpower and pull yourself out of this. You cannot afford to get stuck here!

2. ***Improbable.*** Gradually you see a glimmer of possibility, though doubts and self-imposed limitations persist. But at least you're willing to entertain the possibility of success.

3. ***Possible.*** As your belief in your capabilities grows, you see solid evidence that achievement is feasible after your first few successful steps. This builds momentum towards your goals.

4. ***Probable.*** In this phase, your belief morphs into solid confidence. It is marked by a commitment to do whatever it takes to realize your vision. By now, you've learned to Master the Minimums and you can see the positive results.

5. ***Inevitable.*** This stage signifies a rock-solid belief in the inevitability of your success. Your commitment to your vision is unwavering, making your success seem predestined.

When you're starting out, Stage 5, "inevitable," may seem absurd. So, begin by looking at what small thing you can do *today* to move you closer to your vision and your final destination over the distant horizon. That's the point of *Mastering the Minimums*.

Believing the Inevitable: An Exercise in Self-Belief

Coaching my children's high school tennis teams has helped me see the transformative power of belief. In practice sessions, we don't just hit balls–we build belief. It's fascinating to see how each player's perception of their ability evolves. Not every kid starts at "impossible," but they all have room to grow in their belief. The real magic happens as they progress from seeing their goals as impossible or improbable, to embracing them as probable, and then accepting them as inevitable.

This shift isn't just about improving their game; it's about changing how they see themselves and what they can accomplish. Self-belief, when nurtured, can lead to extraordinary outcomes.

It's important to know where you stand in the stages of belief–to recognize your current mindset and work consciously to elevate it. If you're hovering at "improbable," your next target is "possible." If you're already at "possible," set your sights on "probable." This progression is like climbing a ladder: each rung represents a new level of belief and performance.

I often share with my tennis team is the importance of ***managing self-talk***. If your inner dialogue is riddled with negativity, it becomes exceedingly difficult to advance towards the stage of inevitable belief. Visualize self-talk as a conversation you'd have with another person. If the way you talk to yourself feels inappropriately harsh with others, reevaluate and adjust your self-talk. The voice that rings loudest in your ears is your own. It's also has the most influence.

Awareness of your belief stage is not just about recognizing where you are; it's about understanding your power to change it. This awareness guides you through the fog of doubt and uncertainty towards the clarity of inevitable success.

Tiger Woods: Unwavering Belief

When Tiger Woods first stepped onto the PGA Tour in 1996, the world of golf bristled with skepticism. Among the doubters was Curtis Strange, a seasoned golfer with two U.S. Open titles and a reputation for his straightforward, no-nonsense approach to the game.

During an interview, Strange asked Woods: "What would make this week in Milwaukee a successful one for you?"

Tiger's response was bold. "To play consistently. Winning would be a sweet bonus."

Strange was taken aback by such confidence and exclaimed, "A victory? That sounds cocky to me. You're saying, 'I can win' at your first pro tournament?'"

Tiger, unfazed, replied with conviction: "I've always believed in winning. Second or third is not my aim. Winning matters."

Strange laughed and made a dismissive comment. "You'll learn," he said, but it did nothing to shake Tiger's composure or confidence.

When Tiger's unshakeable belief met the seasoned skepticism of an established golf icon, Tiger proved that strong self-belief could defy expectations and redefine what's possible in golf. Tiger, a prodigy who had been honing his skills since childhood, had amassed an impressive record in amateur golf. His journey was not a series of lucky breaks but a path marked by dedication, skill, and an unwavering belief in his abilities. He knew he could win golf tournaments, one stroke at a time, by Mastering the Minimums.

Months later, Tiger silenced his critics by clinching his first PGA Tour victory. This triumph was the start of a legendary career marked, as of 2024, by eighty-two PGA Tour wins and fifteen major championships. His journey is evidence of the power of self-belief and vision.

Practice "Believe As If to Become"

Every big win in my life began with a blend of audacity, grounded vision, and belief. When my aim was to run a tennis club, I didn't just daydream about it. I asked, "What would the best-of-the-best tennis director do?"

Then, I mirrored that in my own private tennis program. I went the extra mile by Mastering the Minimums: alerting parents with texts if their kid missed a lesson, giving constructive feedback to help young players up their game, and showing up at tournaments just to root for them–all on my own dime.

Securing the role of a tennis club director at age twenty-four was transformative. I always thought I could make it happen, but there was some pesky doubt. Breaking past that doubt was more than a personal win; it changed the game in my closest relationships. My wife, who's always had my back, found a new level of faith in me. She told me this victory elevated her confidence in our shared goals and my ability to make even bigger things happen.

How did I do it? I homed in on each day's tasks, meticulously sculpting my tennis program one calculated action at a time. I was Mastering the Minimums day by day.

To put this principle into practice, visualize your future self with your success already attained. Imagine the feeling of achieving your goals and having a lifetime of wonderful memories. Then, start acting as if you've already achieved them. Ask yourself, "What would my *future self* do in this situation?" and strive to align your decisions and actions with that vision.

As you practice **Believe As If to Become**, your belief in your ability to achieve your goals will strengthen and you'll make longer strides towards your vision. With a potent blend of desire and belief, you can shape your destiny and achieve your dreamed-of success.

Warren Buffet's Clarity of Belief

It was 2008 and the Great Recession was looming. Warren Buffett, a titan in the world of finance with a staggering net worth of over $100 billion, faced the worst crisis of his career. The world economy was crumbling, Lehman Brothers had collapsed, and panic seized the markets. Buffett's Berkshire Hathaway company was hemorrhaging value–over $25 billion annually. Even seasoned analysts questioned whether the Oracle of Omaha had lost his touch.

Buffett, however, never wavered from his foundational principles of consistency and discipline. In the eye of the financial storm, he did something many considered foolhardy: He invested $5 billion in Goldman Sachs. It was a bold move that shocked Wall Street.

Buffett's philosophy has always been about the long game, so he doubled on consistency instead of retreating in crisis. He remained firmly committed to value investing, buying high-quality companies at low prices and holding onto them.

And what was the outcome? That $5 billion investment turned into $10 billion by 2011, providing much-needed liquidity to Goldman Sachs and stabilizing the U.S. financial system. Berkshire Hathaway recovered the $25 billion loss and soared to new heights, reaching a peak market value of $702 billion in 2020. Buffett continued with his lifelong commitment to reading and self-education, dedicating several hours daily to broadening his knowledge base.

Amid all this, Buffett never compromised his simple lifestyle–still living in the same Omaha house he bought in 1958 for $31,500 and still enjoying his junk food and sodas. His relationships remained strong; his family ties were unbroken. He has always said, "It's not about being the smartest person in the room. It's about being the most consistent."

In Buffett's world, consistent actions yield consistent results. Whether it's a financial crisis or the temptation to deviate from our core principles, his story shows that unwavering consistency is the key to withstanding the harshest trials. Warren Buffet has achieved what he wanted to achieve in life and has plenty of wonderful memories!

Embrace Your Future Self

Embracing your future self is a profound introspective journey. It requires understanding and accepting the person you will become. This isn't just about mimicking the habits of successful individuals. It's about internalizing their essence–their core values, beliefs and habits.

What drives your future self? For example: If you see yourself as a confident public speaker in the future, beyond practicing speeches you must embrace the mindset of a confident speaker by understanding and overcoming the fears and anxieties associated with public speaking. It's about building a narrative where you see yourself as confident and capable.

Nurturing your self-belief is about building a relationship with your future self and gradually becoming your future self from the inside out. This journey is about more than just achieving goals. It's about aligning your identity with your aspirations.

- *Understand and accept your future self.* Recognize who you want to become and accept this vision as a part of your identity. It's not just about setting goals or developing skills. It's about seeing your future self as an integral part of who you are now.

- *Internalize the essence of success.* Adopt the actions, the mindset and the emotional resilience of the person you aim to be. This means adopting your future self's core values, beliefs, and driving forces.

- *Make emotional and psychological shifts.* Navigate the emotional and psychological changes that accompany personal growth. Understand and manage the fears, anxieties, and mindset shifts that are part of evolving into your future self.

- ***Build a narrative of confidence and capability.*** Cultivate the mindset of confidence, overcoming fears and anxieties related to public speaking. Create a mental narrative where you view yourself as confident and capable.

- ***Embrace the internal journey and relationship with your future self.*** This involves building a relationship with your future self; understanding the fears, motivations, and mindset; and gradually integrating these aspects into your current self.

- ***Transform your identity to align with your aspirations:*** Make a profound internal shift in how you perceive yourself. Align your current identity with the person you aspire to become and integrate this vision into every aspect of your life.

Doubt: Roadblock on the Path to Belief

The journey from dreaming to achieving isn't merely about the steps we take or the strategies we employ. It's profoundly tethered to the stages of belief that form our mental foundation. These stages of belief shape our resolve, fuel our drive, and ultimately determine our success. It's a dance of determination and doubt, where every step counts.

Initially, when you set a goal, there's a natural high and a strong sense of "I can do this." It's a powerful feeling, full of energy and determination. But then doubt creeps in. It doesn't barge in loudly; it sneaks in quietly, eroding your confidence and shifting your focus. It's like stumbling over a small rock on a sprint. It doesn't seem like much, but it can throw you off your stride.

As doubts accumulate, the effects can be subtle but devastating. They can create a wedge between you and your goal. That robust initial belief slowly starts to crumble and the narrative shifts. You might think, "Maybe I'm not cut out for this," or "This dream is bigger than I imagined."

Doubt is like a sneaky thief stealing your resolve. If unchecked, this downward spiral continues. The fewer actions you take, the weaker your belief becomes. It's a vicious cycle where belief morphs into "it's impossible for me..." and suddenly you find yourself back at the dismal first stage of belief. You look at your castle and see a hopeless task.

This transformation isn't about your capabilities; it's about allowing distractions to cloud your vision and steal your time. It's like letting a pickpocket into your home.

Breaking this cycle requires recognizing that ***doubt erodes belief***. A shift in perspective can make all the difference, treating distractions as minor diversions and threats to your self-belief. It's time to guard your dream like a lion guards its pride.

Ultimately, your belief journey is an inner compass. Internal doubts and external distractions can have devastating effects. By safeguarding your time and mental space from them, you move closer to your goals and fortify your belief that you have what it takes to make your vision a reality regardless of the obstacles. Belief requires an unwavering commitment to your dreams, even in the face of doubt and ridicule.

Doubt Is the Antithesis of Belief

Doubts are like weeds in a garden. If left unchecked, they can choke the strength of our belief in our vision. In our quest to embody the "Believe As If to Become" principle, doubts pull us back into our current state and make it difficult to inhabit the reality of our future selves mentally.

When I began focusing on my future self, doubts and distractions were constant companions. Each time I started to act "as if," the curse of doubts, the lure of distractions, the tug of pending chores, or the pull of old habits tried to pull me back into the comfort of the present.

I realized that this resistance wasn't just robbing me of time; it was eroding the foundation of my belief in my future self.

Consider acting "as if" as a form of mental theater. Immersion is vital for the performance to feel real. Once pulled out of character, an actor can find it hard to dive back into the role. Likewise, distractions can yank us out of our envisioned future and make it challenging to re-immerse ourselves.

Acting "as if to become" is powerful because when we act "as if," we're not daydreaming but building neural pathways that align with our goals. This is *neuroplasticity*–the ability of your brain to re-wire itself with new, positive habits that replace old, negative habits. All decisions and actions that align with our future self strengthen these pathways. Over time, they become our default state. The more we pull ourselves into this mindset, dismissing distractions and reinforcing our envisioned future, the more tangible and achievable our goals feel.

It's like rehearsing for a big play. You learn your part one word, one line at a time. You Master the Minimums. The more you practice, the more fluent and natural your performance becomes. Your brain becomes so wired that you can say your lines without conscious thought. When it's time to step onto the grand stage of your envisioned future, you do so with ease and confidence because, mentally and emotionally, you've been there countless times before.

The potency of the "Believe As If to Become" principle lies in consistent practice, devoid of distractions as much as possible. It's one small victory after another. Minimizing disruptions creates fertile ground where your beliefs can root deeply, grow, and eventually bear the fruits of your desires. Embracing the mindset of your future self, and frequently rehearsing that role undisturbed, sets the stage for a transformative journey from dream to reality.

Mindset and Mastery: Making Vision and Belief Real

Once I watched a video featuring two high school basketball players. After a player flubbed a crucial game move, his body language signaled self-recrimination. Sensing this, his teammate offered a gentle nudge of encouragement, reminding him to maintain confidence and to check his negative self-talk. That single interaction brought about a visible transformation, reinforcing the idea that self-talk influences action.

The term 'mindset' refers to our beliefs, attitudes, and thoughts, which shape how we interpret and interact with the world. It dictates how we handle challenges, process feedback, and make decisions.

In her book *Mindset: The New Psychology of Belief*, Carol Dweck notes that a mindset can be either "fixed," implying an unchangeable set of abilities and characteristics, or "growth-oriented," where there is an understanding that abilities can be cultivated through effort and learning. A growth mindset embraces learning opportunities and views learning as a continuous journey.

Your mindset, along with your belief in your vision and abilities, play a vital role in whether you Master your Minimums. Mastering essential elements becomes arduous if belief in your vision is missing. When you maintain belief in your ability to achieve your vision, Mastering the Minimums seems possible and likely.

As you examine your belief in your vision, where are you in the stages of belief? Your goal should be to improve that belief. If you are at "impossible," what can you do to move to "improbable?" The key to moving through the stages of belief will always be mindset! If your belief is, "This can *never* happen for me," then start working on telling yourself, "This *could* happen," or, "Other people have made this happen, so why not me?"

Bolstering your belief in your vision takes time, patience, and practice. Your path might have twists and turns, but the destination is worth the journey. Moving through the stages of belief won't happen overnight, but as you continue to practice your growth mindset, you will gradually strengthen your belief in yourself and your vision.

Jim Carrey: The Transformative Power of Self-Belief

From sweeping floors in a small Canadian town to sweeping audiences worldwide, Jim Carrey's journey is proof of the power of unwavering self-belief. Born into a family grappling with financial hardships, Carrey's early life was far from the glitz and glamour of Hollywood. At age sixteen he dropped out of school to work as a janitor, helping his family make ends meet after they lost their home.

Carrey's belief challenge was overcoming his circumstances and a series of failures and rejections. His initial attempts at comedy were met with harsh criticism; in fact, comedy clubs often echoed with jeers and boos, not applause. The rejection letters he received were constant reminders of the distance between his reality and his vision. For many, this would have been the end of the road; but Carrey did not give in to defeat.

The turning point in Carrey's life was as dramatic as his performances. He wrote himself a check for $10 million for "acting services rendered," dating it to Thanksgiving, 1995. This wasn't just a whimsical act but a declaration of his self-belief. Carrey carried this check in his wallet, a constant reminder of where he was going. Despite the setbacks he continued to refine his act, learning from each failure and gradually building his resilience. He built his dream castle one stone at a time and worked through both good weather and bad.

The resolution of Carrey's struggle came with hard-earned success. His breakthrough role in *Ace Ventura: Pet Detective* was not just a career milestone but the culmination of years of perseverance. By 1995, when he had dated his $10 million check, Carrey's vision materialized when he earned $10 million for his role in *Dumb and Dumber*. His salary leaped from a janitor's wage to $20 million per film, and he went on to win a Golden Globe with his films grossing over $5 billion worldwide.

Lessons for us. Carrey's story is a profound example of the human spirit's capacity to overcome adversity. This young man from a small Canadian town refused to let circumstances define him. His journey from sweeping floors to becoming a global comedy sensation is a testament to the power of belief and vision, reminding us that no dream is too big if you're willing to pursue it relentlessly, step by step, armed with belief and resilience.

Carrey chose the road less travelled. He faced daunting hardships, from dropping out of school to working as a janitor and living out of his car in Hollywood. His path was riddled with rejection and failure, yet he persisted. Despite its challenges, Carrey's choice to embrace the rugged path of his desires led him to extraordinary success. He didn't just dream; he acted, persevered, and overcame.

Imagine Standing at a Crossroads

Imagine standing at a crossroads in your life. To your left is a path that is rugged, uncharted, and daunting–a path where each step is a leap of faith, a journey through the unknown. This path, illuminated by the radiant glow of your desires, is fraught with obstacles and challenges. It's a path that demands courage, resilience, and an unwavering belief in yourself. Despite its daunting nature, this path is vibrant with the allure of promise and potential. The less-traveled road leads to fulfillment and the realization of your dreams.

To your right lies a different path. It's the easier route, familiar and comfortable and dimly lit by the flickering lights of distractions. This path offers the immediate comfort of gratification, the seductive ease of the known. It's the path of least resistance, where each step is predictable and safe. However, this seemingly comfortable alley is deceptive. It may lead to stagnation, a place where aspirations wither and dreams fade into the obscurity of the mundane.

This is the essence of what it means to choose the path of your desires and your dream castle. It's about facing the hardships, embracing the challenges, and persisting through the setbacks. It's about daring to venture into the unknown to pursue your dreams.

> *Two roads diverged in a wood, and I–*
> *I took the one less traveled by,*
> *And that has made all the difference.*
>
> *– Robert Frost*

As straightforward as it might seem, many of us tend to follow the crowd without pause for self-reflection. We seldom stop to ask ourselves those crucial, life-directing questions, even though life constantly presents us with various crossroads. So, when you find yourself at such a juncture, pause and consider: which direction will I take? The decision you make can significantly shape your life's path.

Action 3: Pick Your Top Priorities

"The key is not to prioritize what's on your schedule, but to schedule priorities."

-- Stephen R. Covey

Now that you've explored the power of "Believe As If to Become," cleared away doubts, and stepped onto the grand stage of your envisioned future, the next action is picking your priorities. You are the architect of your own journey. Every step taken, every priority set, becomes a stone in building the castle that represents your unique journey.

The story of **Chris Gardner** reveals the importance of having the proper priorities in life.

Chris Gardner's Pursuit of Happiness

Chris Gardner's journey from having no home to becoming a big name on Wall Street shows a story of true grit and never giving up. In the 1980s, Gardner, a single dad, was out on the streets of San Francisco with his young son. With only $1,200 and no college education, things looked really tough. His biggest worry wasn't just finding a job; it was keeping his son safe and happy.

The hardest part of Gardner's fight was his dream to make it big in the tough world of stockbroking while making sure his son felt loved and taken care of. They spent nights in subway stations, bathrooms, or anywhere they could sleep. Chasing his dream job was scary because he didn't want to let his son down.

But Gardner kept at it and finally got a break when he passed his big test and got a job at Bear Stearns. This change wasn't just about getting more money; it was about all the hard work, sticking to it, and believing in himself paying off.

From these tough times, Gardner not only made it in finance but also became a symbol of hope for others in tough spots. He started his own company, Gardner Rich & Co, in his apartment. His story of going from no home to success has touched many people, through his book and the movie "The Pursuit of Happyness."

Chris Gardner's life shows how powerful it is to keep going, have a clear goal, and never stop believing in yourself. His rise from being homeless to having millions shows it's not just a story of getting rich but a lesson on the strength of the human spirit to beat the odds with hard work and determination.

Lessons for us: Chris Gardner's narrative is more than a rags-to-riches tale; it's a powerful lesson in prioritizing. It's a vivid reminder that no matter how daunting life's challenges may be, we can overcome them with a clear vision and unwavering determination. His journey from the depths of poverty to the pinnacle of success is an example of the power of aligning our actions with our values, goals and priorities.

Benefits of Setting Priorities

A compelling study from the *Journal of Personality and Social Psychology* provides hard evidence that having clear priorities can boost our sense of purpose and meaning in life and assist us in making intelligent, informed decisions. The study, entitled "Scarcity and Intertemporal Choice," involved over a thousand participants and revealed that eighty percent experienced a notable increase in life satisfaction when they defined and pursued clear, actionable priorities.[i]

The benefits of setting priorities extend beyond just feeling good. Another groundbreaking study, published in the *Journal of Health Psychology*, delves deeper into the impact of prioritization. Over several years, researchers observed that individuals who put their health first–through regular exercise, balanced nutrition, and effective stress management–reported a fifteen percent decrease in chronic illnesses and showed a twenty-five percent improvement in physical and mental health indicators compared to those who let health take a backseat.

Align Priorities with Vision

Priorities direct our time and energy towards what holds the utmost importance. With clear priorities, we become more productive, efficient, and effective in achieving our goals.

Our health may not be a priority until we realize that we are overweight and out of shape. Once we acknowledge this, we can align our desires with our priorities. By establishing clear priorities and Mastering the Minimums, we can improve our health and fitness.

Without well-defined priorities, we risk spinning in circles and feeling exhausted, overwhelmed, distracted, and confused. We may waste time on insignificant tasks, overlook essential relationships, or fail to progress towards our vision.

Your priorities may differ from those around you. It's easy to get caught up in the expectations of others, but ultimately you are responsible for your own life and must prioritize accordingly. As Paulo Coelho once said, "When you want something, all the universe conspires in helping you achieve it." When you prioritize what matters most, you are more likely to achieve your goals because your priorities align with your vision, passion, and action.

Setting Priorities That Stick

Your vision should inform your priorities, guiding you towards what matters most to you. For example: If you dream of being an NBA star, basketball should occupy a top slot in your priorities. Such focus isn't unique to aspiring athletes–it is a universal truth. Whether you aim to be an exceptional parent, spouse, or artist, realizing your dream requires focus on your priorities–perhaps even an obsession.

Basketball all-star Kobe Bryant once said, "I have nothing in common with lazy people who blame others for their lack of success. Great things come from hard work and perseverance. No excuses."

Setting priorities is the linchpin in boosting your productivity and achieving your goals. When you are committed to your vision, your actions automatically align with your priorities. Your level of commitment will largely determine your level of success–and commitment comes from vision, which then transitions into beliefs and actions.

Doubts, distractions and setbacks gain power when your priorities are murky. For example: If becoming a public speaker is low on your priority list, every setback can trigger self-doubt, derail your vision, and even make you abandon your goal. But when your vision and priorities align, stumbling blocks become stepping stones. Having clear priorities helps you dodge distractions and turn "failures" into lessons learned on your path to greatness.

Think of your life as a blockbuster movie where you are both actor and director. Your priorities are the script. A bad script turns a promising production into a flop. But with a solid script every scene takes on meaning, bringing you one step closer to that standing ovation.

By scripting priorities, you direct your actions towards fulfilling your dreams and desires.

DIE WITH MEMORIES NOT JUST DREAMS

Viola Davis: Picking Your Priorities

The life of actress **Viola Davis** shows us what can happen when we navigate our life by the script of well-chosen priorities.

In 2015, Viola stood at a life-altering fork in the road. On one hand, the ABC drama *How to Get Away with Murder* extended a once-in-a-lifetime role that promised to catapult her into stardom. On the other hand, she was in the middle of adopting a child–a deeply personal and emotionally charged process. The stakes were enormous. Both roles demanded her full attention and neither role would wait.

The pressure was crushing. For Viola, this wasn't merely about balancing work and family; it was a seismic choice that would define the kind of person she would be. Would she be the actress who broke barriers but couldn't escape the set to be with her child? Or would she be the mother who put family first, turning her back on a potentially career-defining opportunity?

Viola didn't choose between the two roles. She integrated them by ensuring that her daughter was with her on set during breaks. This wasn't a compromise, but a bold redefinition of what success looked like for her.

The impact was immediate and measurable. Viola Davis became the first Black woman to win the Emmy for Outstanding Lead Actress in a Drama Series. Her performance was critically acclaimed and shifted cultural conversations. She was also a hands-on mother, rewriting the script that says you can't chase career ambitions *and* be an involved parent.

Viola's dual priorities produced personal milestones and paved the way for broader dialogues about diversity and inclusion in Hollywood. Her actions illustrated the unyielding power of clear, uncompromising priorities.

CLARIFY WHAT YOU WANT

Lesson for us. In today's fast-paced world, pinpointing priorities and deciding where to direct our time and energy can be daunting. Several responsibilities and roles demand our attention. It's easy to swamped and uncertain about our priorities. However, having a clear vision and strong aspirations can help us to channel our time and energy towards what truly matters most.

Be Honest When Identifying Priorities

As you identify your top five priorities, I urge you to be honest! When you list your priorities, you may be tempted to make a popular list designed to please others because you want to be seen a certain way or you see yourself in a certain way. Don't do this! Your priorities are *your* priorities. Don't ever change them for other people's approval.

My top five personal priorities align with my vision, simplifying the commitment process, guiding me as I allocate my time and resources every day, and informing the actions that I seek to master.

Here they are:

1) God

2) Family and community relationships

3) Health

4) Business and career

5) Hobbies.

Those are my priorities. They may not, and need not, be yours.

73

Charlie: Recognize Your Authentic Priorities

Once I had a client named **Charlie** who was very committed to his business; in fact, he once bailed out of a family trip to handle some urgent work matters. I made no judgment of him. It was his castle and he was building it the way he wanted.

When he made his priority list for me, he listed his business at number five.

I challenged him, saying, "I know you! There's no way your business is number five. It is either one or two!" We discussed his priorities and why he put other things before his business.

Charlie thought that I would judge him and think he was a terrible husband and father if he put work as his top priority. But I already knew that business was his priority and I supported him one hundred percent.

After our talk, he threw away the fake list and created a new one aligned with his real priorities. From there, he and I created an action plan that made sense for him. He said it was the first time he could be honest about what was most important to him in his life at the time and not feel ashamed about it.

Our Priorities Shift Over Time

We're all busy. But we all somehow make time for the people and things that matter to us now, in the season of life we are in. A new mom once told me that her life wasn't great because she couldn't do things that her older sisters were doing. She wanted to go out to lunch and spend hours with friends. She was resentful about having a newborn and feeling tied down.

Life is a series of chapters, each with unique challenges and opportunities. Whether you're a new parent, launching a business, or caring for aging parents, recognizing your current life phase will help you home in on immediate priorities without feeling guilty or resentful.

Our priorities shift as we navigate different stages, face new challenges, and grow. What's crucial today might take a backseat tomorrow as other aspects of life demand our attention. This fluidity is the natural rhythm of life and acknowledges that we're multifaceted beings with evolving needs and aspirations.

Your priorities are like stock prices–they fluctuate based on market conditions. There's no such thing as a "perfectly balanced life." One area will always scream for more of your focus. Life will always be a little unbalanced. The balance will come over time when priorities shift, and your attention swings to areas that you may have pushed aside earlier.

Avoid the pitfall of designating *everything* as a priority. That's unrealistic and a surefire way to spread yourself too thin! List your top five priorities to show you what matters most now.

Having more than five priorities is akin to having none at all. What's your top priority? What's your number five? Identifying your priorities and listing them in order can be challenging since many things constantly vie for your attention.

Your number five priority often represents one that you have temporarily set aside or put on hold. It's not about neglect; it's about strategic placement or postponement. Other priorities naturally drift into the background as you focus intensely on specific top priorities.

But these sidelined priorities are not forgotten. They're simply waiting for their turn in the spotlight. I am paraphrasing, but I have heard John Maxwell say, "Having more than five priorities is akin to having none at all."

For example: When career development takes center stage, hobbies or leisure activities might take a back seat. This doesn't mean they're unimportant, but rather they're in a holding pattern. Over time, as your primary objectives are met or evolve, those other areas can be brought back into focus.

The bigger picture, and more balanced narrative, will emerge when you look at your life as a whole rather than as isolated segments. Periods of intense focus are balanced by times when other aspects of life get their due attention. It's like a well-orchestrated symphony—each section has its moment to shine, contributing to a harmonious overall experience.

Once your priorities are selected, you can create an intelligent **action plan** to help achieve your vision. For instance: A massive study from 1969 to 1980 dissected how goal-setting impacts performance. The study found that when people set specific and challenging goals, their performance and engagement skyrocket. They are thirty-three percent more likely to surpass their own records than when their goals are vague or too easy. And when these goals align with what truly matters to them–their core values and priorities–the impact is even more profound.

Aligning your goals with your heart's true north enables you to break through barriers, as my life demonstrates. When I align my goals with my priorities, I achieve things that once seemed like pipe dreams.

In high school and college, I never read a single book outside of class because reading for personal development or enjoyment wasn't a priority at the time. But in my twenties, my priorities shifted and reading became important to me. Despite being a slow reader, I committed to a Minimum daily reading action and maintained consistency.

The result is that in the past fifteen years, I have read or listened to over a thousand personal development books. Studying these books and implementing the insights improved my attitude towards reading. Previously, I was cynical about the power of reading. But the more I read, the more my mindset evolved, and this challenged my preconceptions.

I started recognizing achievable patterns and concepts by prioritizing personal development. I developed new aspirations, experimented with concepts, and personalized them. And then I started *writing* books! I became an author! This is how powerful your vision and priorities can be.

We often take the time to review our grocery lists, plan vacations, and organize our weekends, but rarely do we apply the same diligence to reviewing our lives. Real-life examples underscore the importance of this practice.

Consider the story of Chris Gardner, whose journey from homelessness to financial success was marked by his relentless focus on a singular priority: creating a stable life for his son. His story teaches us the power of having clearly focused priorities.

Similarly, J.K. Rowling's path to becoming one of the most successful authors in the world began with her prioritizing her passion for storytelling, even while facing financial hardships and rejections. Her unwavering commitment to her craft, despite the obstacles, highlights how prioritizing what truly matters can lead to unprecedented achievements.

These stories, along with countless others, illustrate the transformative power of understanding and aligning with our priorities. They serve as a reminder that, whether it's committing to career goals, personal development, or family, the clarity of our priorities directly influences our capacity to achieve our dreams.

Reflect on what truly matters. I encourage you to sit alone, free from distractions, and reflect on what brings you joy and what you regret. These emotional highs and lows can unveil your true values and assist in establishing genuine priorities.

For instance, my greatest joy comes from traveling with family and friends, creating lasting memories and sharing experiences.

Conversely, my deepest regrets stem from times when work took precedence over family, leading me to miss important moments with my kids.

Recognizing what brings happiness and regret has been crucial in shaping my values and living by them. However, reaching this level of understanding and alignment with my priorities required making sacrifices. It meant reassessing commitments, sometimes scaling back on professional obligations, and reallocating time and energy to what mattered most.

This journey wasn't straightforward; it demanded tough choices and trade-offs to truly align my life with my values.

Seven Steps to Picking Priorities

Now, how do you identify and act on your priorities? Here are my seven steps:

1. ***Reflect on what truly matters.*** I encourage you to sit alone, free from distractions, and reflect on what brings you joy and what ends in regret. These emotional highs and lows can unveil your true values and assist in establishing genuine priorities.

   For instance: My greatest joy comes from traveling with family and friends. This is how I create lasting memories and shared experiences. Conversely, my deepest regrets stem from times when work took precedence over family, leading me to miss important moments with my kids. Recognizing what brings happiness and what brings regret has been crucial in shaping my values and living by them.

   However, reaching this level of understanding and alignment with my priorities required making sacrifices. It meant reassessing commitments, sometimes scaling back on professional obligations, and reallocating time and energy to what mattered most. This journey wasn't straightforward; it demanded tough choices and trade-offs to truly align my life with my values.

2. ***Eliminate the noise.*** In today's digital age distractions are just a click away, constantly clamoring for your attention. You have to make conscious decisions to filter out the unimportant noise by muting unproductive social media or setting specific periods for scrolling. Don't let the noise limit your life. Ignore the noise that interferes with building your castle.

3. ***Visualize your future.*** When you visualize your future, you show yourself what is possible. You can sit for a few minutes daily and ask yourself where you see yourself in five, ten, or twenty years. Identify the people, experiences, and achievements that are in your vision. This helps you realize the action you must take to make it happen.

4. ***Find your trusted confidantes.*** More than just friends, confidants are trusted people who can offer insight because they see things from a different perspective. They have your best interest at heart and give you straight talk. These people can also be accountability partners. Their perspective will serve as encouragement and provide tough love when you need it.

5. ***Write your priorities.*** Writing your priorities makes them like a commitment contract. Since your priorities are constantly shifting, you need to reevaluate them regularly. You may find that your number-five priority has shifted to the number-one spot for a season. Reevaluating helps you stay focused on and aligned with your evolving vision.

6. ***Act on your priorities!*** Avoid diluting your focus by labeling everything a priority. Again: When everything is a priority, nothing is. Listing priorities without acting on them is a nice academic exercise. But if you want a castle, you need to build it action by action.

7. ***Review and repeat.*** Prioritizing is a process of constant renewal. That's why it is vital to prioritize learning and growth. Whether through books, online courses, coaching or mentorship, you should work on what you are learning as you set your priorities and act on them. The more you learn through action, the more you grow.

Be Honest: Align Your Priorities and Actions

If you list your business as priority number five when it is actually number one, due to perceived judgments, you create dissonance between your actions and your true priorities. By being honest with yourself and shedding the fear of judgment, you get in sync with your heart's desires.

Some people will judge you no matter what. If you're overweight, they'll say you're lazy. If you're skinny, they'll say you're bulimic. Judgment is unavoidable. So why tailor your priorities based on the distorted judgments of others?

One of the best things you can do for yourself is overcome your fear of judgment. Setting your priorities on your terms helps you reclaim your narrative. Be audacious. Be bold. You're the master of your castle, the guardian of its gates. Permit only the worthy to reside within.

And when life happens, practice self-compassion. Mistakes and missteps are par for the course. When you stumble, pick yourself up, reevaluate your priorities, and stride forward revitalized. Listen closely to the subtle cues of your innermost interests; they're your most trustworthy navigators. Rumi said, "Be quietly drawn by the strange pull of what you truly love."

The next time someone gives you a side-eye for your life choices, just smile and think, "I've got places to go, dreams to achieve, and zero time for your unsolicited opinion of my life."

> *"Friends and family typically will not start supporting you until strangers start celebrating you!"*
>
> *– Jefferson Green*

DIE WITH MEMORIES NOT JUST DREAMS

SECTION 2

BUILD MOMENTUM

In Section 2, you are invited to take three more actions to build momentum towards realizing your vision.

Action 4: Take Action and Master the Minimums

Action 5: Create and Celebrate Win Streaks

Action 6: Design a Supportive Environment

Action 4: Take Action and Master Minimums

"A journey of a thousand miles begins with a single step."

– Lao Tzu

"The magic is doing the simple things repeatedly and long enough to ignite the miracle of the Compound Effect."

– Darren Hardy

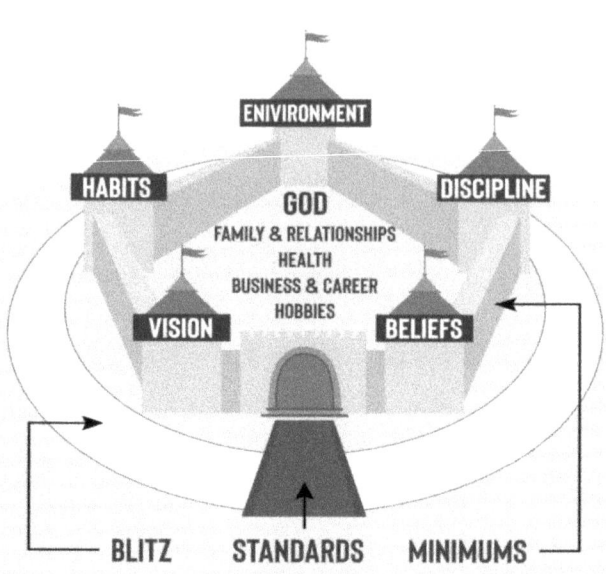

Building your dream castle requires taking focused actions with three different degrees of intensity or duration: Minimum (non-negotiables,) medium (Standard) and maximum (Blitz) actions. These correspond to the walls (Minimum,) the drawbridge and gate

(Standard,) and the moat (Blitz.) While Minimum actions keep your core intact, Standard actions ensure growth and Blitz actions lead to quantum leaps.

Minimum actions are the small consistent actions you do daily, without fail–actions such as eating a healthy diet, getting regular exercise, getting enough sleep, earning money, and serving other people. Their cumulative impact cultivates discipline, accountability, and consistency for long-term success. These actions constitute the non-negotiable priorities. They are what you do, even on your most challenging days and weeks.

Standard actions are more substantial, like putting a roof on your castle or installing the drawbridge. They're important and expected, but not done every day. Standard actions are larger tasks you aim to complete regularly. These actions build momentum and make substantial progress towards your aspirations while maintaining some semblance of balance.

Blitz actions are life changing. They correspond to rebuilding a part of your castle damaged in a storm, or adding a new wing because your family is growing. In your life, they're like changing careers or getting married. Blitz actions require planning and extra resources. Blitz actions are intense bursts of effort to accelerate progress towards specific milestones. These actions build confidence and propel you closer to long-term aspirations

Lance Learns to Master the Minimums

When my friend **Lance Conrad** reached his early forties, he had become a dynamic public speaker and was appearing before thousands of people worldwide. He was happy with his life and career because he had met many of the goals he had set for himself years earlier. He was making a six-figure income, traveling worldwide, was applauded by his appreciative audiences, and generously compensated by his grateful clients. He had an incredible relationship with his wife, Tanya, and his three daughters.

One day, he had a revelation that changed his life. At one of his speaking events, while on stage, Lance glanced up at the big screen behind him and thought: "That guy is FAT!"

Then Lance blinked in surprise, realizing that he was the overweight figure! And the jarring realization that he had barely recognized himself wouldn't leave him.

Later, in his hotel room, Lance reflected on how he had neglected his health and fitness in the pursuit of business success. The shocking image of himself on the big screen was a stark contrast to the person he once knew. Over the years, without noticing, he had let himself go. He no longer felt the vitality that used to define him; his energy had dipped, and he found himself feeling sluggish more often than not. His wardrobe had gradually changed, too, accommodating his new size, a silent testament to the shift he had ignored.

This moment of realization was Lance's wake-up call. Having once prioritized physical fitness, he was now faced with the consequences of his neglect. How had he strayed so far from his own standards?

Over time, Lance had taken one step after another away from the place he wanted to be. It was as if, after building a fine castle to live in, he had become distracted by his career and failed to do the **_Minimums_** to maintain his health. He had substituted one set of values for another. His inner and outer demons were tearing down his castle.

Lance had been fit and even athletic for most of his life. But as his speaking career soared, the relentless cycle of fast food meals, constant travel, and exhaustion became the routine pattern of his life.

These small things that came with life on the road took him further away from his health goals–his body castle–and now these damaging distractions were being manifest physically.

In a way, Lance was lucky: he had a wake-up call before it was too late. He had been chasing dreams rather than building memories. We all need dreams of a better life. Without dreams, we languish. So, we also need to Master our Minimums by taking small steps in the right direction.

When Lance told me of his dilemma I listened, understood his situation, and saw the distractions in his life. I knew I could help him in this particular area. He realized he had been ensnared by the subtle traps that had started to consume his well-disciplined life. In many ways, he had crafted a life of discipline and success. He just needed assistance with his health and fitness.

So, I guided him towards a ***simple fitness regimen***. I helped him identify and navigate the unique challenges of maintaining his physical wellbeing while enjoying his high-flying lifestyle.

When we began planning his physical fitness program, Lance humorously claimed, "Rob, I'm allergic to working out!" Though he laughed, it was clear that this "allergy" was a mask for something more profound. After all, Lance had once been a competitive athlete. He knew what it took to be fit, but his pursuit of professional excellence had taken precedence. Late-night meals, fast food, and neglect crept in, eroding his physical well-being–the fine castle that he had carefully constructed, stone by stone, during his younger years.

The enormity of regaining what he had lost intimidated Lance, not because he doubted his ability but because he couldn't see the starting point. His fitness once flowed from competitive sports but that was no longer an option. The idea of hour-long gym sessions seemed daunting.

Lance needed to create **Minimum standards** for his health and even more specifically working out. So, we began with a clear objective: ***don't miss!*** I told Lance, "I don't care how long you spend at the gym. Just don't miss." The notion of *not missing* can translate into an attainable Minimum target, like dedicating fifteen minutes to aerobic exercise or weight training twice a week. Once you set your Minimum, no excuse and no slacking is allowed.

Lance had an exercise routine on his phone that he could follow in his hotel room. Lance was free to enjoy as much healthy food as he desired, but not to indulge in junk food between meals. And he was never to step on a scale to weigh himself. This plan was not about a number, but about feeling good and being healthy.

I was confident he could achieve this Minimum because I knew he would swiftly notice the benefits. He would become more alert, sleep better at night, and have more energy. The positive results would be evident.

Over the next few months, we slowly increased his Minimums. He exercised thirty minutes several days a week. The key was that he set out to follow the Minimum of just showing up at the gym to work out even if he tricked himself into believing it would be for just ten minutes. He wasn't going to miss a week of working out and he was going to try to work out several times a week.

Almost always, those gym workouts where he may have not felt like working out, or only intended to work out for ten minutes, led to much longer workouts. He became healthier. His old clothes fit again. He had to buy a smaller belt for his pants.

Stone by stone, he rebuilt the fine castle he had neglected. And as Lance lost weight and improved his health, he set a goal to run fifty miles and ascend twelve thousand vertical feet across the Grand

Canyon's rim. He ran marathons, Tough Mudder challenges, and Spartan races. His consistency with the Minimums enabled him to focus, exceed expectations, overcome perceived limitations and distractions, and bring new energy to his personal life and his business.

When he and I discussed one upcoming race, I asked him, "Can you even fathom the person you've become compared to the 'Fat Lance' version of yourself?"

He laughed and replied, "Absolutely not. This version of me was beyond what I imagined!" I now joke with Lance and tell him he took my advice way too seriously! Lance is in his mid-fifties and in the best shape of his life.

Lessons from Lance

Lance's story resonates with us because it reflects our hopes, dreams, struggles, and victories. The start of his new life was **Mastering the Minimums**. He wouldn't be where he is today without committing to minimal progress. Mastering the Minimums enabled him to create a win streak and eventually create a version of himself that was beyond what he imagined.

Think about this deeply. When you Master the Minimums, you create a win streak. When you create a win streak, you begin to change how you see yourself. When you begin to change how you see yourself, you create a new identity, which creates true change.

Change doesn't have to be complicated or require intense struggle. It comes from focusing on **simple, consistent steps**. Instead of tackling everything at once, getting sidetracked, and quitting from discouragement, you can focus on simple, consistent actions. When you consistently act towards your vision, your reality will eventually surpass even your most ambitious dreams.

Lance suffered not because of one catastrophic illness or event. He didn't wake up one morning fifty pounds overweight. He got there by taking many small steps, one by one, away from his dream castle. Because he was absent, his castle deteriorated one stone at a time. Demons–inner and outer–preyed upon it. To rebuild it, he simply reversed the process. He took small steps, one after the other, back to where he wanted to be. He rebuilt his castle one stone at a time.

Your path might be unique, but the progressive principles are universal, timeless, and proven. They're quickly and readily available to anyone willing to embrace them.

If you have set ambitious goals and become engrossed in your pursuits, only to fail or have other areas of your life suffer because you lost sight of maintaining essential balance, remember: You can reclaim what you lost, spark profound transformations, and achieve and sustain success by adopting a positive mindset, by believing that positive change is possible, and by focusing on the right consistent actions. You *can* change, regardless of how old you are, where you live, or how much money you have.

Yes, you have unique challenges and obstacles. But that doesn't give you a "pass" on owning your life and showing up for others. You can conquer the demons and distractions in your life once you adopt a positive mindset, decide what you want, and reclaim the path to success.

Master Minimum Actions

"The way to get started is to quit talking, begin doing."

– Walt Disney

"The secret of getting ahead is getting started."

– Mark Twain

Yes, it is true: you won't get anywhere until you get started. So, start with Minimum actions.

Mastering the Minimums is a powerful method. Instead of being overwhelmed by the end goal or sidetracked by minor distractions, zeroing in on one small non-negotiable step or task at a time keeps the momentum going. Instead of being paralyzed by the extensive journey ahead, you anchor your actions in the Minimums.

These seemingly tiny and trivial actions form a protective barrier against distractions. They are doable, not daunting. Focusing on the Minimums helps you refocus your attention and reminds you why you are doing this. Over time, Mastering the Minimums creates a cascade effect of positive habits that lay the groundwork for your success.

Every physical transformation is a testament to our ability to push past external and internal distractions and find the path to personal success. By Mastering the Minimums, you make the first step manageable; from there, you can build upon your success.

Success boils down to focusing on small, consistent actions. It's the antithesis of grand failure-setting strategies. Have you ever been on the "tomorrow diet?" You'll start eating great tomorrow, but tomorrow turns into tomorrow again? Doing the Minimums flips the script.

This concept has guided countless individuals towards discovering their purpose and taking action to live out their purpose. We all have a purpose; our job is to find and live it–to die with wonderful memories, not wasted dreams.

Try It Before You Knock It

When I share my secret to physical fitness success, some people expect a strict diet regimen and a six-hour-a-day exercise plan. But I tell them:

The secret to success is *Mastering the Minimums*–the basics that can and must be achieved no matter what life throws your way.

You, too, may scoff initially at the idea of doing the Minimums to lose weight and rebuild your castle, but I invite you to try it before you knock it.

Please let me share a personal example. I'm not the most athletic person, but I'm in good shape because I've Mastered the Minimums–the basic actions I do daily, whether traveling, unwell, or not feeling up to it.

For instance: My Minimum for working out is thirty minutes three times a week. I can do it because I make time to do it. Do I sometimes have to give up something to meet my Minimum workout requirement? Yes. We cannot do it all. We all need to prioritize.

You may be picturing success without recognizing the essential Minimum steps. By focusing on the Minimums, you find a simple and manageable starting point–perhaps to commit to fifteen minutes of exercise twice weekly. You may doubt that fifteen minutes of exercise twice a week will improve your health and help you lose weight, especially if you think that change requires crazy amounts of work and sacrifice. It doesn't–just commit to the Minimums.

You may struggle at first, but when you stick to your Minimum actions you overcome distractions and self-doubt. Over time, you begin to Master these Minimums. Without anyone forcing you to do so, you begin extending your gym time, increasing intensity, and adding extra days. Your success in meeting your Minimum goals leads to more confidence and ambition.

Simply Do the Basics Better

The principle of *Mastering the Minimums* can be applied to any aspect of life, a testament to the power of starting small and consistently **doing the basics better**.

Your Minimum depends on your current condition and goals. For example: When **Michael Phelps** was training for the Olympics, his Minimum was swimming 80,000 meters a week. That's nearly fifty miles. He practiced five to six hours a day, six days a week, and more if he was training at altitude.

Your Minimums are like the stones that you pile up, one at a time, to build your castle and its towers. Alone, each one may seem insignificant; together, they are formidable.

While action is at the heart of progress, *reflection* and *evaluation* serve as its soul. As we progress, we need to pause and assess: What actions yield results? Periodic evaluation ensures you're not just busy, but productive; not just moving, but progressing; not just efficient, but effective. Periodic reflection enables you to appreciate the castle you're building.

Remember: Every vision begins with a dream and every dream can become a vision, which materializes through each action, decision, and discipline you make to bring your vision to life.

So, when you desire to lose weight, you need not create a restrictive meal plan and daunting exercise regimen. You just need to *Master the Minimums* by taking small, consistent steps like working out for fifteen minutes a few times weekly. Soon your entire identity is transformed and you can't imagine skipping workouts.

Minimum Actions Alter Your Identity

For actual, lasting change, you must have an ***identity change***. The Minimums are the best way to create that identity change. Achieving grand visions for your future demands consistent effort and dedication over time. You must Master the Minimums!

Minimum non-negotiables represent actions you commit to performing daily or weekly, without exception. These actions should be achievable regardless of how you feel or what life throws your way. By committing to these Minimums, you establish a foundation of consistent effort that propels you towards your aspirations even during moments of wavering motivation or overwhelming circumstances. Even on your most challenging day, when battling a job loss or financial hardship or a medical condition, you can still stay committed to your Minimums.

If you frequently travel for work and want to maintain a regular exercise routine, your Minimum could be getting fifteen minutes of exercise three times a week. This might involve a quick hotel room workout, a run outdoors, or some yoga in your hotel room with a towel as your mat. Committing to the Minimum ensures progress towards your fitness goals.

I haven't missed a personal development day in the past fifteen years, largely because my Minimum for personal development is simply reading or listening to something. For you, a Minimum action might be a slow walk toward your destination. A Standard is a jog, whereas a Blitz goal is a full sprint. There are times in life to walk, to jog, and to sprint.

Given your commitments and the dizzying whirlpool of 'urgent' notifications, you can easily lose sight of what's essential. So ask yourself: Amid the chaos, what tiny but mighty forces could work silently in my favor? Forget the applause, the spotlight, or the viral hit. Think about your Minimum non-negotiables, because they are the backbone of your life.

Setting Your Minimums

Everyone wants to go for the huge, crazy goal. It sounds big and bold, but often they miss the steps in between. They forget that grand achievements are built on small, consistent efforts.

Mastering the Minimums can turn those lofty dreams into manageable, achievable goals. Yes, you want to go bigger, faster, stronger! But first master the small, consistent actions to meet your goal.

Your Minimum actions should either be daily or weekly commitments within your control. For example: Consider setting a weekly commitment to exercise at least once. Likewise, reading personal development content could be a daily Minimum. These Minimums are action-based commitments, not results-oriented aspirations. For example: Shedding fifty pounds could be your objective but the Minimums outline the steps you'll take to achieve this vision.

Setting your Minimum actions around your goals is all about consistency. You will have bad days, weeks, and maybe even months. Your Minimum actions are commitments or promises you're willing to uphold and honor, even on your worst days, with the exception of personal or family emergencies and accidents.

To maintain commitment to Minimum actions, you need to overcome thoughts like "I don't feel like it," "I'm too busy," or "This isn't important." When you feel off-balance, overwhelmed, or doubtful, your Minimum actions will buoy you up.

So, consider: what commitments are you willing to keep, consistently, even on your worst days? If you can't commit to Minimums, you'll never reach your goals. Your dream castles are built with consistency. The things you do or don't do repeatedly have consequences, for better or worse.

When my kids complain about not wanting to do something, I remind them: If you don't brush your teeth one day, you may have bad breath or some other minor consequence. And if you continue not brushing your teeth, the consequences will impact your life. You may need dental work or even lose your teeth!

Minimums are all about committing to take consistent action daily or weekly. It is crafting a life based on your vision and priorities. Show me your Minimums and I'll forecast your success.

Why Write Your Minimums?

I encourage you to write your Minimums. A study by Dr. Gail Matthews at the Dominican University of California found that people who write their goals are forty-two percent more likely to achieve them! I also encourage you to cultivate a "no matter what" mindset. This mindset enables you to stay true to your commitments–to do what you say you're going to do when you say you're going to do it. Embracing this mindset helps you to stay focused on the journey, not just the destination. It's not only a mantra; it's a science-backed mindset that empowers you to stay aligned with your intentions and take steps to achieve your big, bold goals.

Now ***create your Minimum action list***. Look at the priorities. What are you willing to commit to on your worst weeks for each of the five pillars? This isn't the time to become Superman or Wonder Woman. It's a time to reflect on weeks when you lost sight of your vision and lacked motivation. Ask yourself, "What would I have been willing to do that week?"

After you write your Minimum non-negotiable action list, ***display it*** somewhere visible–in your bathroom, bedroom, office, refrigerator or phone. And think of a phrase or affirmation you will tell yourself each evening when you've accomplished your Minimums. It can be something like, "I kept the streak alive," "Mission accomplished," or "Progress, not perfection." Find words that resonate with you and acknowledge that you've fulfilled your commitment.

Medium or Standard Actions

"Vision without execution is hallucination."

– Thomas Edison

Standard actions encompass consistent actions that challenge you but remain feasible. These actions require discipline because they are like the drawbridge of your castle, fortifying your vision and safeguarding your priorities. A Standard action may be entering a 5k footrace or going on a long hike. You don't do it every day, and so it's a challenge, but the feeling of satisfaction you get from doing them is invaluable.

Shackleton: Story of Remarkable Endurance

In the early twentieth century, **Sir Ernest Shackleton** embarked on a harrowing and daring expedition to be the first to cross the entire continent of Antarctica. Shackleton's ship, the *Endurance*, set sail in 1914, but disaster struck when the ship became trapped in ice.

As the *Endurance* was slowly being crushed by the shifting ice, Shackleton and his crew were forced to abandon ship and survive on the frozen wasteland of Antarctica. They faced extreme cold, harsh conditions, and the constant threat of starvation.

Their unwavering Standards of courage, perseverance, and camaraderie kept Shackleton and his crew going. Shackleton refused to let his men give in to despair. He maintained a sense of purpose and kept their spirits high, reminding them of their survival duty.

The crew endured unimaginable hardships for over a year, from camping on ice floes to navigating treacherous waters in lifeboats. Despite the odds, not a single member of the crew perished.

Shackleton's leadership and unwavering Standards of survival saw them through.

Ultimately, they were rescued, and their story became one of history's most extraordinary tales of survival. Shackleton's Standards of resilience and teamwork turned a seemingly insurmountable disaster into a triumph of the human spirit. Shackleton's adherence to his Standards of leadership enabled the survival of his crew and made him a legend.

The lesson from Shackleton's story is this: ***even in the face of extreme adversity, your Standards and unwavering commitment to your goals can lead to remarkable feats***. Your Standards, like Shackleton's, can be the guiding force that helps you overcome the most daunting challenges and achieve your goals no matter how impossible they may seem.

Stick to your Standards to perfect them. They will be your compass in the most challenging journeys.

Standards: Engines of Breakthrough Success

Standard actions require more deliberate discipline, focused effort, and energy. These actions will propel you towards your vision, but they often require additional time, resources, or strategic planning.

For example: If your goal is to start your own business, your Standard actions might include networking with potential clients or partners, conducting industry research, developing a comprehensive business plan, and creating your product or service. These actions require a higher commitment than Minimums, but they are essential to realizing long-term aspirations.

My personal development *Standard* is to read for thirty minutes each day. While I strive to meet my Standard, I have my Minimums as a fallback when travel, other obligations, or unexpected events arise. The also applies to my workout routine. My *Standard* is to hit the gym for one hour, five days a week. I navigate my daily life using Minimums, Standards, and Blitzes. My Standards enable me to make the most of my day and ensure consistent growth.

When you start your journey towards your vision, you focus first on Mastering the Minimum to build momentum and stay committed to the process. Early wins fuel our dedication. Once you Master the Minimums, you can set your Standards. Soon you will be doing your Standard actions most of the time.

To make Standard actions work for you, prioritize them and incorporate them into your schedule. These actions should become a regular part of your routine to ensure consistent progress towards your aspirations.

When determining your Standards, think about your ideal day. What would it look like if you could accomplish everything you desired? While every day won't align perfectly with that vision, reflecting on it will help you identify your Standard actions.

The power of Standard actions can lead to unimaginable breakthroughs. It's not just about the end goal but the journey, the iterations, and the unyielding perseverance that genuinely illuminate the path to success.

Committing to Standard actions establishes a foundation of consistent effort that propels progress towards your aspirations. Even when you lack motivation, taking Standard actions allows you to move closer to your vision. Over time, these consistent efforts will enable you to achieve your aspirations and create your desired life–your dream castles.

Maximum or Blitz Actions

"Massive action cures fear."

– David Schwartz

Sometimes you need to step up and tackle a significant task or project that takes more than a day or two–a task that carries significant value. It's like putting a new roof on your castle, or digging the moat, or adding a new wing.

Blitz actions are like secret weapons in your life's arsenal. They are dedicated bursts of intense action accelerating growth and bringing you closer to living your vision. They represent the moat of your castle, a testament to unwavering commitment.

Blitz actions can take different forms. They could happen once a week for a few hours, perhaps once a month for three days, or even once a quarter. The key is their intensity and the leap they propel you to make towards your goals. Since you don't take Blitz actions often, they are challenging; but you gain deep satisfaction for achieving a real milestone.

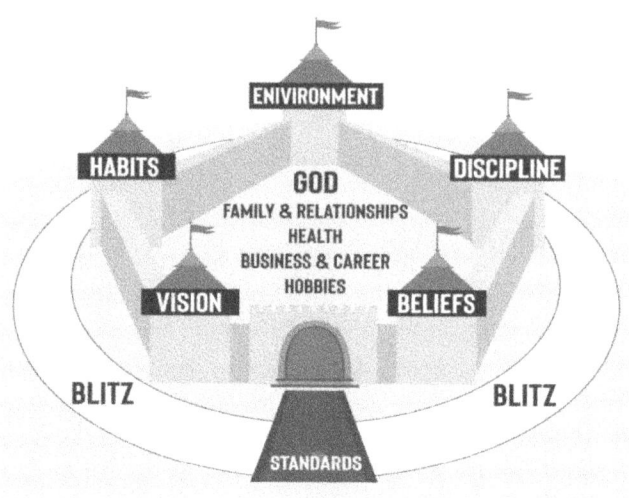

For instance: A Blitz action might be a week-long endurance hike, getting a big promotion, having your first child, starting your own business, enrolling in medical school, or relocating to another city or country.

The word *blitz* means *lightning*, suggesting that the event happens quickly. But it may take time. While taking a Blitz action every quarter may yield results, without consistent Standard actions and non-negotiable Minimum actions your progress will only reach a certain point before burnout sets in and excuses start to prevail.

Tony Robbins Needed a Blitz

In the early 1990s, **Tony Robbins** stared into the abyss of bankruptcy. His empire, Robbins Research International, teetered on the edge and was hemorrhaging money.

Rather than pull back, Robbins leaned into the storm. He needed a *Blitz*–a daring, audacious move that would either propel him into legend or send him crashing. With his back against the wall, Robbins announced an outlandish goal: $9 million in sales. Not in a year or quarter, but in ninety days.

The tension was palpable. His team scoured every lead, revitalized dormant partnerships, and put in eighteen-hour workdays. Robbins led the charge, accelerating his seminar schedules and crisscrossing the country to host events. He was not just walking on hot coals; he was sprinting. They launched an aggressive marketing campaign and flooded TV, radio, and print–all while orchestrating live events for thousands. The atmosphere was electrifying but draining.

Tick-tock, the clock counted down. The room on day ninety was a cauldron of mixed emotions. The calculations began and the revenue numbers rolled in: They hadn't just met the $9 million mark. They had blown past it.

This *Blitz action* saved the company. Robbins Research International surged in value and Robbins solidified his reputation as a titan of personal development.

Since then, Robbins has carried the ethos into every venture. He's hosted events with over 200,000 attendees in a single year, launched bestselling books, and amassed over a million podcast listeners. The Blitz tactic had become a part of his DNA, transforming Robbins from just another motivational speaker into an international force.

Robbins didn't just dodge a bullet. He caught it in his teeth and shot it back. Through Blitzes, he pivoted from the edge of disaster to a trajectory aimed at the stars.

The lesson for us? ***When you're up against the insurmountable, the Blitz isn't just an option; it's the only solution***.

Guts and Glory of Blitz Action

All high achievers benefit from Blitz actions–taking concentrated, high-intensity efforts for durations to achieve major milestones or aspirations. A Blitz action may embody a real *risk* offset by a potential big reward. In contrast, Standard and Minimum actions carry little, if any, risk.

Blitz actions demand a laser-like focus. They may require you to step outside of your comfort zone and take calculated risks. They may involve launching new products, initiating projects, or reaching out to potential clients or partners. A Blitz could also be massive attention to any type of relationship in need, whether it's your parents, kids, or spouse.

When you use Blitz action and dedicate intense effort to advance in a specific area, you find yourself temporarily imbalanced. Your aim is not to remain imbalanced, but to gain momentum and leverage growth during the Blitz to achieve the vision and priorities that matter most to you.

By taking Blitz actions, you risk a major failure. Actively seeking opportunities to fail sounds counterintuitive, but you learn and grow faster. As John Maxwell says, "Fail forward faster."

One of my clients struggled with a declining sales team. She feared that her business was going under and leaving her stuck.

Instead of fearing failure, we reframed the objective. We incentivized the sales team and told them whoever received the most "no's" would get a prize. This unconventional approach turned the situation into a game, igniting their motivation and driving sales. The sales team wasn't afraid of rejection anymore–they were *looking* for it.

This is a powerful example of how rejection was reversed into an incentive. My client's sales team gained momentum when we set up this "No" Blitz.

Blitz action involves dedicating a specific period of time to go all-in on a particular goal or project. That's why it goes above and beyond both Minimum and Standard actions. The time frame can vary–it may be a day, a week, or–in extreme cases–a month. Finding a balance is critical so that your Blitz action doesn't eclipse other essential aspects of your life.

My Experiences with Blitzes

I've done many Blitzes myself. For example: I might go hard for three to seven days for personal development reading. When elevating my fitness game and eating habits, I've extended these Blitz periods to a month twice a year. There's no one-size-fits-all Blitz; you need to find your own sweet spot and perhaps break or bend some rules.

Recently I went on a three-month health Blitz with my workout buddy, Adam Gerulat. It's the longest health-focused Blitz I've tackled in seven years, and it was intense. The goals I set were audacious. When you've got big ambitions, you need more time to climb that peak.

Each Blitz is a learning experience, and over time they build confidence and generate momentum. As you plan your Blitz, remember that, like any tool, it's all about how you wield it.

Suppose you want to run your first marathon. Scheduling Blitz action for the marathon may mean setting the dedicated time on a weekend to run further than you run during weekdays. It may mean pushing yourself to exhaustion to run faster than usual.

During Blitz action, eliminate distractions and interruptions and focus wholeheartedly on the task. Also, involve your loved ones in your plans. Ensure they understand that your full attention will be restored after the Blitz, to gain their support and minimize the strain on your relationships. It's easier for the people in your life to support you when they know they will get back your time and attention.

Too often, we set the vision and say, "Someday, when this happens, and I have worked myself to death, it will be worth it." In the process, we lose the people closest to us because we take Blitz action for too long and miss out on being with them. Don't let this be you.

Before you race into an adrenaline-fueled Blitz, I caution you to not get *too far* out of balance. Blitzing is as much about preserving what you hold dear as it is about pushing your limits. Don't be the racer who, in a quest for speed, forgets to refuel. You need to navigate the emotional terrain.

I always let my family know whenever I set up a Blitz action plan. I will talk with my wife and kids and tell them what I am trying to accomplish, how long it will take, and what's in it for them. This always leads to having my family on board when I take Blitz action.

For example: I might say to my family, "For the next two weeks, I will work towards making five big sales for my business. This will require working extra time on the weekends. I won't be able to make all of the activities you have scheduled, but I will make sure to be available to tuck you in at night. And when I finish this Blitz, we will celebrate by doing a fun family activity."

The more I include the people closest to me, set expectations, and communicate what is happening, the more on board everyone will be. When your family and loved ones see how important the Blitz is to you and to them, they are willing to make sacrifices.

Navigate the Highs and Lows of Intense Focus

When you complete the Blitz, reflect on your actions, analyze the results, make necessary adjustments, and follow up with potential clients or partners to capitalize on your efforts. Without followup, you fail to gain and utilize valuable feedback and insights. Embrace failures as stepping stones towards growth and make the most of the lessons they provide.

Blitz actions enable you to achieve your vision and milestones within a condensed timeframe. These actions challenge you to step out of your comfort zone, take calculated risks, and make major progress towards your long-term aspirations–your vision and priorities.

Think of Blitz actions as a reset button or reboot for your life. At times, we're so entangled in the web of distractions that our daily Standard-action routine feels like having dozens of browser tabs open. We constantly switch between them, never focusing on or finishing a task. Taking Blitz action is like closing all unnecessary tabs and focusing on one essential task, thus making the system run smoother and more efficiently.

This focused approach can detox the distractions that have plagued you. It's like a fast from the routine of eating. In health and fitness, intermittent fasting allows the body to cleanse and rejuvenate by taking a break from constant digestion. Similarly, Blitz action grants our minds a break from the noise of modern life and gives us space to target and eliminate a specific challenge.

For instance: Imagine an aspiring writer bogged down by the demands of a nine-to-five job, social media distractions, and a bustling social life. He wants to write a novel but never manages to start. By initiating a Blitz action, he sets aside a dedicated weekend, or an entire week, cutting out all unnecessary social media engagements and dedicating himself entirely to writing. He progresses on fast-forward with his aspiration and discovers the joy and passion of uninterrupted creation.

Or take the case of a business owner caught in the daily grind. A Blitz action could mean a short retreat–away from meetings and operational hassles–to focus on business development. This retreat is not a vacation but a targeted time to break free from the distractions.

Blitz action is potent in breaking the chains of prolonged distractions because it offers a dramatic change of pace. When we get stuck in a rut, we often need a powerful jolt to our system. When a car is stuck in mud, you can't slowly push it forward. You need to get a tow truck to yank the car free so you can go on your way.

Blitz action is the wake-up call that resonates deep within us, reminding us of our capabilities, passions, and desires. It's proof of our resilience, showing that we have the innate capacity to rise, focus, and conquer even when distracted for extended periods.

Blitz action is not about being reckless or impulsive but about making a strategic, high-intensity push towards our goals. By periodically taking Blitz actions, we make fast progress, reaffirm our commitment to our aspirations, and rediscover the passion that got us started.

Remember: ***Building your dream castle requires taking focused actions with three different degrees of intensity or duration:*** Minimum, medium (Standard) and maximum (Blitz.)

Action 5: Create and Celebrate Win Streaks

"I've missed more than 9,000 shots in my career. I've lost almost 300 games. Twenty-six times, I've been trusted to take the game-winning shot and missed. I've failed over and over and over again in my life. And that is why I succeed."

– Michael Jordan

Creating and celebrating win streaks is the secret sauce to accelerating your progress, as many accomplished people can attest, including comedian Jerry Seinfeld.

Jerry Seinfeld's Three Actions

In the early 1990s Jerry Seinfeld was already a well-known professional comedian, but he wanted to be a *legend*. He felt that he needed to do something radical to break free from the comforting cycle of moderate success. He came up with a daily writing routine where every day, he wrote at least one new joke. No exceptions.

Jerry got himself a massive wall calendar and started marking it with **red Xs**. Each X represented a day he had written fresh material. The chain of Xs grew longer, and so did the pressure.

One night he faced a pivotal moment: the most agonizing writer's block. A deadline loomed for a significant gig. His reputation was on the line and his wall calendar haunted him.

Fueled by his commitment to Minimum actions, Jerry ripped through the block. The gig was a triumph and the chain of Xs was unbroken.

This wasn't just about writing jokes. His daily actions impacted other areas of his life–punctuality, focus, and business acumen. The result was astounding. Jerry Seinfeld's average gig attendance spiked by forty percent within two years and sold-out shows became his Standard. His refusal to let adversity beat him led to sustained success.

The Blitz action came with *Seinfeld*, the bold TV show that was "about nothing." By 1998 it had become the most profitable sitcom, pulling in $3 billion in syndication. In 2005, Comedy Central named Jerry the twelfth greatest stand-up comedian of all time. His show *Comedians in Cars Getting Coffee* broke new ground, amassing over a hundred million views in its first six years.

Again, the through line for all these monumental achievements is Mastering the Minimums, rolling out the Standard actions, and even going for the Blitz–and winning every time.

The Power of Consistency

When we hear stories of famous personalities, we tend to forget that their success didn't happen overnight. Behind their achievements lie countless days of sticking to their Minimums and days when they pushed forward even when being pulled back. Their stories prove that while grand accomplishments capture the spotlight, the small consistent actions build the foundation.

In pursuing your goals, recognize the ***power of consistency***. No matter how lofty, every dream is built brick by brick, action by action. By practicing this principle, we shield ourselves from the snares of distractions and set the stage for unparalleled success. And as we journey forward these consistent, Minimum efforts light the path, ensuring that our dreams aren't just figments of imagination but milestones waiting to be achieved.

The magic of Minimum actions happens in their consistent application. You may be pulled in by fad diets or the allure of quick-fix solutions, but it's your Minimum actions–the ones that you commit to do even in the most challenging times–that transform you. You will only consistently move forward when you consistently move forward.

Ask any athlete, artist, or entrepreneur. Their climb to the top wasn't a straight-shot rocket ride; it was a series of steps, many so small that they might have seemed inconsequential. But these consistent Minimum actions compounded over time into massive results.

You might wonder, "If they're so powerful, why isn't everyone focusing on them?" We often believe we're stagnant if we're not making huge strides. But a building stands tall because of its foundation, not its facade.

Your Minimum actions are that foundation. So, the next time you are tempted to miss or dismiss your Minimum actions, remember to celebrate small wins. Every check on that calendar, every small decision to stick to your non-negotiables, is an act of defiance against distractions, inconsistency, and mediocrity.

There are times to walk, times to jog, and times to sprint. If you only attempt to have success by sprinting, you will burn out. So, choose to run the marathon in a world that's running sprints. Set your pace, maintain consistency, and watch as those Minimums create massive success. Remember, it is not just the intensity but the consistency of your actions that fulfills your aspirations.

So, embrace the power of Minimums, resist distractions with unwavering commitment, and build an unbeatable ***win streak*** of success. Becoming your best self is about being the most consistent. It's about showing up every day and taking the small steps that lead to leaps and to legends! The key to having win streaks is choosing attainable actions on your busiest or most challenging days. These actions should be small enough to ensure you can accomplish them no matter what, yet significant enough to move you closer to your aspirations. It's through small and simple steps that great things come to pass. Setting Minimum non-negotiables helps you show up consistently. It builds momentum and confidence, cultivates a mindset that embraces consistency and self-commitment, ***and starts a winning streak***.

DiMaggio's Amazing Hitting Streak

Joe DiMaggio, the legendary baseball player who played for the New York Yankees, achieved one of the most remarkable feats in baseball history by hitting safely in fifty-six consecutive games. His hitting streak remains unbroken today, a testament to his exceptional skill, dedication, and ability to create his own personal win streaks.

DiMaggio's hitting streak was not a stroke of luck or a coincidence. It resulted from his disciplined approach to the game and unwavering commitment to improvement. DiMaggio was known for his meticulous preparation and attention to detail. He would spend hours practicing his hitting and fielding skills, constantly striving to refine his technique. He understood that success in baseball, like any other endeavor, required consistent effort and focus.

But DiMaggio's streak did not start with fifty-six consecutive games. It began with a single game where he hit safely once. He built upon that small win, staying disciplined and focused on the process. Each game was a chance to extend his streak, and he approached each at-bat with determination and purpose. DiMaggio's win streak serves as a potent reminder that sustained success is the result of consistent, intentional action over time.

Creating your own win streak requires setting challenging aspirations and committing to consistent action aligned with your vision and priorities. It starts with defining your Minimum actions that provide a foundation of consistency and help build momentum towards your goals, just as DiMaggio's single hit in the first game of his streak paved the way for fifty-five more.

DiMaggio once said, "I'm just a ballplayer with one ambition: to give it all I've got to help my ball club win. I've never played any other way." He created a win streak by keeping this at the top of his mind. He committed himself to excellence every day.

Remember, during his long career he had several hitting streaks! When he would be on a twenty-day streak, and he failed in game twenty-one to get on base, he wouldn't spend weeks whining about it. The next game, he would start day one of his new hitting streak and see how far he could take it.

Mindset of Maintaining Win Streaks

Our mindset plays a crucial role in creating and maintaining win streaks. We often struggle with getting started on tasks. We overestimate future motivation and succumb to procrastination. We can overcome these challenges by breaking down aspirations into small actionable steps and cultivating a positive mindset. Maintaining a positive mindset allows us to stay motivated and disciplined, even when we don't feel like taking action.

In my life, I have experienced the power of win streaks. Whether reading personal development books, praying, working out, or making sales calls, starting with Minimum actions has led to transformative win streaks. It was a challenge to stay committed sometimes, but the momentum and sense of accomplishment from keeping the win streak alive pushed me forward. Even small actions, when done consistently, can significantly improve our lives.

Sustaining win streaks is vital to long-term success. You build win streaks with a series of small victories. Admiral William H. McRaven tells the story about soldiers and sailors making their beds every morning. This little task is important because many recruits come from difficult backgrounds. Some have never made a bed. In the service, the first thing they do every morning is make their beds. This requirement gives them a small sense of confidence and of a "job well done."

Making your bed every day may sound silly. But for many raw recruits, completing this simple chore, day after day, without fail, represents a small but meaningful win streak. It's another stone in their castle, which they place every day. If you miss a day and snap your win streak, then don't look back. Begin again. Start over and keep building.

Win streaks are not immune to setbacks and challenges. They often require us to overcome obstacles and weather storms along the way. However, maintaining a positive mindset and staying disciplined in our actions helps us push through these challenges and emerge stronger on the other side. By facing adversity head-on and staying committed to our aspirations, we can overcome obstacles and keep our win streak alive.

Imagine standing at the base of a giant hill, peering up at its looming peak. The ascent seems insurmountable. But then you take that first step and another. With each stride the path gets slightly more accessible and you realize that your momentum is building.

This is the essence of win streaks–making progress, gaining momentum, celebrating each win, and powering through, turning small victories into monumental triumphs.

Making Relentless Progress

Win streaks are not just about tallying numbers, but embodying a spirit of relentless progress. It's about lighting the fire of ambition, feeling it burn brighter with each accomplishment, and turning it into an unstoppable blaze of determination. Every time we add to our win streak, we're not just adding a notch to our belt. We are broadcasting a loud and clear message to ourselves: "I am capable, I am resilient, and I am on fire."

The thrill of a winning streak is electric. Each consecutive win is like the beat of a heart-pumping song that keeps us dancing, moving, and craving more. And the longer the streak, the more intoxicating the rhythm becomes. It's like a drug, where each achievement, each ticked-off task, gives us a hit of dopamine and fuels our desire to push the boundaries of our capabilities.

Win streaks are infectious. As you ride your wave of success, others begin to notice. Your enthusiasm, dedication, and unwavering commitment become a beacon, lighting up a path for others to start their win streak. It's a ripple effect where your energy, drive, and persistence inspire those around you to chase their dreams with renewed fervor.

A win streak of Minimum actions will embolden you to tackle more challenging Standard actions; and if you build up a win streak of Standard actions, you'll have the confidence to take on a Blitz action! It's like being a manager. If you can successfully manage a team of ten people for a year (Minimum action,) then you'll be ready to manage a department of a hundred people (Standard action.) If you can build a win streak doing that, then you'll be ready to be the CEO of a company with a thousand employees. Minimum wins facilitate Standard wins and then Blitz actions.

Yet every win streak must come to an end. The end streak is a moment of reflection, a chance to recalibrate and learn the experience's lessons.

Instead of seeing a broken streak as a failure, we can see it as a pit stop–a chance to refuel, reassess, and restart with a new burst of energy.

The magic of a winning streak lies in the spirit of persistence it fosters. It's about bouncing back with twice the zeal, harnessing lessons from challenges, and sprinting to new victories.

Start Your Own Win Streak

Before you kick off your journey towards success, hold onto T. Harv Eker's insight: "Every master was once a disaster." Begin your win streak with a mindset geared towards continuous improvement. Allow this pursuit to push you forward, finding satisfaction in the hurdles overcome and the progress made. Experience the fulfillment that comes from shaping a victorious narrative. Transform your goals into a sequence of triumphs, each marking your relentless dedication. Keep in mind that every noteworthy achievement starts with a single victory and it's time for yours to take shape.

Creating your own win streak is a transformative journey that can bring you closer to your aspirations and help you achieve sustained success. It starts with setting clear and challenging goals, taking intentional actions aligned with your vision, and maintaining a positive mindset. As you embrace the process and stay committed to disciplined action, you unlock the power of win streaks and experience their transformative impact. So, set your Minimum actions, stay focused, and get ready to create your own remarkable win streak.

I love to track progress. Win streaks are a great way to do that. They help us see how consistent we can be, and losing a winning streak has data for us to learn from.

Think about the last time you had a winning streak going and what made you lose that win streak. Did you get sick? Did you tell yourself no one was saying "yes" to the sales call, or you just "didn't feel like it?"

When I lose a winning streak, I ask myself, "What happened?" With those two words, I open up a wealth of feedback I can learn from. Don't be ashamed of losing a winning streak; learn from it!

Disney: The Alchemy of Action and Mindset

Walt Disney faced his darkest hour when his first studio, Laugh-O-Gram, went belly up. Most would've seen bankruptcy as the end of the line, but not Disney. With only $40 in his pocket, he headed from his hometown of Kansas City to Hollywood. "If I'm going to risk everything," he thought, "let's make it in a place built for dreamers."

In Hollywood, he and his brother Roy founded Disney Brothers Studio. This was where Disney set his triple-action strategy into motion: Minimum, Standard, and Blitz actions.

The first involved small but consistent steps. He committed to creating one new animated short every month. Within a year those twelve animated shorts garnered him a fan base that exploded to over a hundred thousand followers, laying the groundwork for what was to come.

For his Standard actions, Disney took a massive leap. Feature-length films including *Snow White and the Seven Dwarfs* and *Pinocchio* were born. These weren't just movies; they were phenomena. *Snow White* alone pulled in an unprecedented $8 million during its initial release–a vast sum during the Great Depression.

Then came Disneyland, the Blitz action that would cement his legacy. The idea for a theme park in Anaheim, California was audacious, even insane to some. The skeptics called it "Walt's Folly," predicting it would go bankrupt within a year. The pressure was astronomical; one wrong move could spell the end of the Disney empire.

But here's where Blitz action came into play. Disney orchestrated short, concentrated bursts of radical moves, from altering construction plans overnight to securing last-minute sponsorship deals that injected crucial funds.

Despite the tremendous challenges, Disneyland opened its doors in 1955 to an unprecedented crowd of 28,000 visitors on the first day. And at the center of the park, visible to all, was–and still is–the magical Sleeping Beauty Castle. Based on the nineteenth century Neuschwanstein Castle in Bavaria, Germany, it created a focal point for the park and excited the imagination of young and old alike. Today, Disneyland hosts more than eighteen million visitors annually.

Disney's strategy of combining Minimum, Standard, and Blitz actions built an empire, and it revolutionized entertainment. Disney risked it all and faced insurmountable odds, but through calculated, varied actions he built a legacy that turned him from a bankrupt dreamer into a symbol of global enchantment.

The Disney strategy is yours for the taking and the playbook has been laid out for us.

Consider **Phil Knight**, co-founder of Nike, who started by selling sneakers from the trunk of his car. He took Minimum actions by making cold calls and securing small-scale retail contracts. Standard actions included expanding into stores. Then came the Blitz: a $1,000 bet with a factory owner to produce a unique sole that became the Nike "waffle" design. Nike's current market capitalization is over $200 billion, and it all started with a series of calculated actions.

Taking Minimum, Standard, and Blitz actions can help you create a rhythm and system for accomplishing your own aspirations. Each type of action serves a unique purpose, contributing to your momentum and creating a winning streak.

Action 6: Create a Supportive Environment

"The environment around you shapes who you are and who you become."

−Tony Robbins

Your ***environment*** is where you nurture your vision and priorities. It's fertile soil for the seeds of your dreams. Creating an environment supportive of your vision is critical to success. We often don't devote enough time to thoughtfully designing and constructing the spaces where we invest our time and energy. A supportive, intentional environment can offer resources, opportunities, and encouragement. Conversely, an unsupportive or hostile environment can obstruct progress and distract from your vision.

Why do you need to create or find an environment that supports your vision and priorities? ***You can't out-discipline a lousy environment***.

Spotlight on Kobe Bryant

There is no better story to spotlight the power of environment than that of the great basketball player, **Kobe Bryant**. At the heart of his legacy lies a battle against the norms of the lifestyle of NBA players and even against his own team's expectations. Despite the widespread notion that partying after games was a rite of passage and a way to unwind, Kobe saw it as a diversion from his singular goal: to be the greatest basketball player of all time.

This difference of opinion came to a head one fateful morning at 4:30 a.m. Kobe's teammates on the Los Angeles Lakers, including LeBron James and Dwayne Wade, stumbled back into the hotel after a late-night escapade. The doors opened as they waited for the elevator, revealing Kobe, in workout gear, drenched in sweat. For a moment, they thought Kobe had been partying; instead, he was returning from an intense practice session. It was his non-negotiable Minimum.

The impact was immediate and profound. A ripple effect surged through the team, flipping their late-night party environment to one of early-morning workouts. The shift was seismic. Productivity during practice sessions soared and injury rates decreased. Player statistics improved, some attributing their first All-Star Game appearances to this newfound focus.

"What you do speaks so loudly that I cannot hear what you say."

– Ralph Waldo Emerson

Kobe's actions exemplified Ralph Waldo Emerson's wisdom. He made a concrete, irrevocable statement through his actions, not his words. The numbers spoke: five NBA championships, two Olympic gold medals, and a legacy that forever altered the sport's course.

Changing pro sports norms wasn't just a win for Kobe. It was a game-changer for every athlete who followed in his footsteps. He didn't just set a new Standard; he demonstrated the transformative power of unyielding focus, indomitable work ethic, and an environment crafted to serve not just talent but a vision for unparalleled greatness.

The Vital Role of Environment

In each area of your life–physical, social, spiritual, mental, or online–your environment plays a pivotal role. So how do you identify what's helping or holding you back?

Do a quick scan of your home, work, and community environments, making a list of triggers that either boost your focus or drain your energy. Your vision needs the right conditions to flourish. So, scrutinize your list and ask yourself: Is this helping me thrive?

Now that you've noted your environmental triggers, how can you craft the ideal environment? How can you create spaces that resonate with your vision intentionally?

During our lean years, my wife and I didn't let financial constraints deter us from creating an environment conducive to our mission. We invested in what mattered. Our environment was great for bonding over board games and fostering meaningful relationships. As our situation improved, we upgraded our lifestyle and expanded our horizons. We began inviting families on trips to create shared experiences and build a supportive community.

Over time, our improved financial situation allowed us to give back in ways we never imagined. We started donating more to our church than we used to earn, a testament to our belief in the power of giving. We also focused on creating more enriching experiences with our kids, understanding that these moments are among the real treasures of life.

Your environment should be as dynamic as you are. It doesn't have to cost you an arm and a leg. Since not every environment will be conducive to peak performance, you must also learn how to operate in less-than-ideal conditions. How can you adapt if you find yourself in a hostile environment? Every environment has its unique rhythm, rules, and energy. These factors can either make or break you. Regularly assess what's working and adjust as needed. Audit your environment to ensure you're aligned with your goals.

Power and Pitfalls of Different Environments

When you are trying to develop a new and innovative product, you need to surround yourself with like-minded but diverse individuals who feel safe to openly share ideas to foster creativity. It's essential to remember, as the saying goes: "If you chase two rabbits, you catch none." This means focusing your efforts on cultivating an environment conducive to innovation rather than splitting your attention between conflicting priorities.

If you are a college student who has aspirations to excel academically but your social circle prioritizes partying over studying, your environment will be a liability. The pressure to conform and "fit in" can overpower even the most vital personal ambitions.

If you spend much time online building your business, you will find the digital world–with its incessant notifications, social media platforms, and endless streams of content–to be a massive distractor.

If you're a writer aiming to complete a novel, you might find that regularly checking email and social media or going down the rabbit hole of unrelated online articles inhibits your productivity. Constant digital distraction leads to fragmented focus and delay in achieving goals.

> *"If you chase two rabbits, both will escape."*
>
> *-- Chinese Proverb*

If you are an athlete training for the Olympics, but your training environment is filled with naysayers, doubters, and critics who tell you that you're not good enough or that your goals are too lofty, your hostile environment might erode your self-belief and affect your performance.

If you are keen to start your own venture but opt to work from your cozy couch, your comfortable environment might hamper your productivity. Soon, you might find yourself taking frequent naps or watching TV because the environment invites relaxation.

These examples illustrate the importance of having a dedicated work environment. Every environment has its vibe. Whether it's the lure of social media in a digital environment, the temptation of a cozy bed in a physical setting, or the sway of a dominant opinion in a social circle, environments matter. They can subtly shape decisions, mold behaviors, and influence outcomes. Creating spaces that support our goals is vital to achieving our aspirations.

Rowling: The Elephant House

Before she became the global phenomenon that we know today, **J.K. Rowling** was a single mom struggling in Edinburgh. Her first drafts of the Harry Potter series were born amid the clamor of coffee shops. But it wasn't until she found the Elephant House–a café with a secluded back room offering views of Edinburgh Castle–that she found her sanctuary.

Despite the serenity, Rowling's journey to publishing her work was anything but smooth. Publishers slammed doors in her face. Naysayers dismissed her vision. At her lowest, she faced the grim prospect of her literary dreams crumbling.

The stakes were high. Rowling had a child to feed and her self-esteem was hanging by a thread. Rejecting the naysayers, she doubled down at her newfound haven and wrote for hours. Her unwavering focus was tested to its limits as she revised drafts and faced mounting bills. The Elephant House was more than a café; it was a fortress where she fought for her dreams.

Fast forward to today. The *Harry Potter* franchise has sold over five hundred million copies worldwide and been translated into eighty languages. It is worth an estimated $25 billion. J.K. Rowling's net worth soared to a billion dollars, becoming one of the wealthiest authors in history. The Elephant House has morphed into a landmark, drawing fans worldwide to witness the room where Rowling's imagination materialized into a cultural titan.

Consider the spaces where you spend most of your time. Do they ignite your creativity or snuff it out? Just as Rowling's Elephant House became a catalyst for her astronomical success, your environment can be a critical factor in achieving your vision. The suitable space will be the stage upon which you perform your most extraordinary acts. Design spaces that amplify your ambitions. You can't climb to the summit if you're stuck in a swamp.

Why do some people seem to be on top of their game every day? Take a look at their space. A tidy environment is like a blank canvas, allowing creativity and productivity to flourish. When your physical area is in order, you're mentally prepared to tackle what comes your way.

Research from the University of California, Irvine, shows that distractions can derail focus, taking the worker an average of twenty-three minutes and fifteen seconds to get back on track. As researcher Gloria Mark noted, "People compensate for interruptions by working faster, but this comes at a price: The experience more stress, higher frustration, time pressure, and effort. Individual differences exist in the management of interruptions. Personality measures of openness to experience and need for personal structure predict disruption costs of interruptions."[ii]

Open offices look cool but can interfere with concentration. A survey by Bospur PR, a San Francisco–based public relations agency, found that seventy-six percent of respondents said that they "hate" open offices, citing a lack of privacy (forty-three percent;) difficulty concentrating (twenty-nine percent;) and an inability to do their best thinking (twenty-one percent.) Many companies once again offer secluded areas for tasks that demand focus.

Change of Venue Causes Gain in Weight

Growing up, I always leaned towards a healthy lifestyle, relishing nutritious foods and constant physical activity. This all changed when I embarked on a two-year mission to Argentina for the church. Amid this new setting, my once vigorous daily routine dwindled, and my diet shifted significantly towards a heavier intake of bread. The transition was insidious, with weight gain creeping up on me so gradually that I barely noticed–until a particularly revealing moment of self-awareness.

Yes, it's a rather personal detail, but the truth hit me while I was sitting on the toilet: I noticed rolls of fat on my stomach for the first time. It was a startling realization that I hadn't recognized the extent of my physical change until that moment. This was the wake-up call I needed. I immediately knew I had to make a change–not only did I cut back on eating bread at every meal, but I also took up jump roping every night as a means to get back into shape.

This pivot back to prioritizing my health wasn't just about shedding the extra weight; it was a reclaiming of my identity and the lifestyle that I valued. Since making those changes, I've committed to a rigorous exercise regimen and a mindful diet that pays homage to my body's needs. I've never looked back. My journey underscores the broader truth about the impact of our environment on health and performance. It extends beyond just the physical spaces we inhabit; it encompasses the habits we form and even the clothes we wear, which, as studies suggest, can significantly influence our psychological processes and, by extension, our physical well-being.

Reflecting on my experience, it's clear that environments deeply influence our actions and, subsequently, our health. Whether it's the sedentary lifestyle I fell into in Argentina or the dietary habits I adopted, the environment played a pivotal role. However, recognizing the need for change and taking action lay entirely within my control.

This story is a testament to the power of self-awareness and the importance of aligning our daily practices with our overarching goals. It's a reminder that while we may not always control the external factors in our lives, we hold the reins when it comes to how we respond and the choices we make towards our health and well-being.

Dwayne Johnson: Emotional and Spiritual Environment

Before basking in the Hollywood spotlight, **Dwayne "The Rock" Johnson** struggled with his demons: crippling depression and anxiety. These demons attacked his castle (which wasn't very big back then!) stole stones, tried to crack its foundations, and poked holes in the roof.

Johnson was drowning emotionally, so he decided to sink or swim in a gym. He was desperate for an outlet, a sanctuary to escape the thunderstorm in his mind. For Johnson, the gym was more than just a room full of weights; it was his emotional rehab center.

Imagine standing at the edge of a cliff, a roaring abyss of emotional turmoil below, questioning your worth and existence. That's where Johnson found himself–alone with anxiety and depression. The conflict was monumental, his very own emotional Everest. The noise in his head got so loud that it drowned out everything else–his dreams, aspirations, everything.

Johnson harnessed the power of physical exercise to bulldoze through emotional roadblocks. His intense workout routine became his therapy session–a practical, data-driven approach to mental well-being. He is so committed that he has a gym that follows him wherever he goes.

In his memoir, *The Rock Says...*, Johnson delves into the importance of self-awareness. He knew that recognizing his weaknesses was the ticket to magnifying his strengths, and so he engaged in emotional engineering. By 2021, The Rock had an estimated net worth of $400 million. He went from a struggling wrestler to a blockbuster actor, producer, and entrepreneur. But his most significant win was his mental and emotional resilience.

Lessons for us: As we craft our physical surroundings to align with our goals, we create a healthy emotional environment that is crucial for our growth, happiness, and well-being. We enhance our ability to manage our emotions effectively. When our emotional environment is healthy, we are better equipped to navigate life's challenges, sustain fulfilling relationships, and find contentment in our everyday lives.

As we gain control of our emotions, we can communicate more effectively, respond to others' emotions productively, and form more profound, meaningful connections. Studies show that individuals with high emotional intelligence often experience less stress, anxiety, and depression.

If you are over the age of thirty, you likely grew up in an environment a lot like mine. Our society didn't talk much about emotions then. Thankfully, we now talk more openly about our emotions and know that it is healthy to experience a wide range of emotions. It's becoming mainstream for men and women to talk openly about our feelings and emotions and to create an environment that boosts our mental, social and emotional health.

Cultivate a Resilient Emotional Environment

Cultivating a positive emotional state involves being mindful of our thoughts, emotions, and behaviors, and maintaining emotional balance. This can enhance our cognitive abilities, problem-solving skills, and creativity–all vital for achieving our goals.

Your emotional environment can also impact your priorities. If you are trapped in an emotional environment characterized by victimhood or constant survival, you will struggle to remain committed to your priorities and fulfill your aspirations. A negative attitude can sabotage your progress no matter how hard you work or where you work. Nurturing a healthy emotional environment will naturally guide your actions in the right direction.

An uplifting spiritual environment can steer our decision-making, inspire us to pursue our passions, and help us perceive challenges as growth opportunities. It can bring us inner peace and clarity, helping us navigate life's complexities gracefully and efficiently. Cultivating a positive spiritual environment can supply us with a sense of purpose, fulfillment, and direction.

From personal experience, I attest that fostering a positive spiritual environment can enhance our relationships. When we base our spiritual environment on values such as compassion, kindness, and empathy, we become more open to others' perspectives and experiences. This can improve our communication skills, build trust, and encourage collaboration in our personal and professional relationships.

Decluttering Mental Space for Spiritual Connectivity

The words of French philosopher and Jesuit priest Pierre Teilhard de Chardin resonate deeply with me: "We are not human beings having a spiritual experience. We are spiritual beings having a human experience." These words urge us to transcend the material realm and connect with our spiritual core to find meaning and purpose in life. They remind us that life's experiences, positive or negative, are opportunities for growth, and that we can find greater fulfillment by connecting with our spiritual essence.

Creating daily spiritual connections encourages inner peace, mindfulness, and personal growth. For me, this comes from studying scriptures, praying to my Father in Heaven, and attending my church and temple. For you, it might look different. Cultivating your personal spiritual environment involves introspection and creating experiences that make you feel part of something bigger than yourself.

By nurturing a positive spiritual environment aligned with your values and beliefs, you can find purpose, meaning, and fulfillment. Your spiritual environment can guide your decisions, improve your relationships, and enhance your well-being.

Ed Mylett, a successful entrepreneur, speaker, coach, and bestselling author, always emphasizes the importance of connecting to a higher power. "True success is not just about achieving material wealth and status," he said, "but also about finding inner peace and fulfillment through spiritual growth and connection."

His words highlight how often people in today's fast-paced world devalue their spiritual growth and development. Cultivating an environment conducive to spiritual growth is essential for achieving inner peace, purpose, and contentment in life. This spiritual environment encompasses practices, beliefs, and values that connect us to our inner self, a higher power, and the world around us.

Self-imposed distractions often reside in our thoughts, becoming stumbling blocks in our emotional and spiritual environments. Often we find ourselves in a spiral of negative self-talk. Thoughts such as "I'm not good enough," "I'll never succeed," or "I don't deserve this," are self-imposed barriers that distract us from our true potential and cloud our spiritual connection.

These inner dialogues can be major deterrents to our success. Just as clutter in our physical environment can prevent us from progressing, mental clutter can divert us from our emotional and spiritual paths. Each negative thought is like clutter, obstructing the clear passageway to our inner selves and our connection to a higher power.

Our minds are frequently inundated with worries, regrets, and what-ifs. These distractions prevent us from being present and rob us of the joys of the current moment. They prevent us from connecting deeply with our emotions and tapping into our spiritual reservoir.

Meditation and mindfulness are tools we can employ to counter these distractions. They help us foster an environment of self-awareness, wherein we can identify these distracting thoughts, acknowledge them without judgment, and gently guide our focus back to the present.

Engaging in spiritual practices–praying, reading scriptures, or connecting with nature–can help silence the noisy chatter of our minds. These moments of spiritual engagement act as a reset, grounding us in our beliefs and values and clearing away the distractions.

Our thoughts shape our reality. Just as we would remove a pebble from our shoe that's causing discomfort, we need to address and eliminate distracting thoughts that hinder our emotional and spiritual well-being. Recognizing these self-imposed distractions and actively removing them not only uplifts our emotional environment but deepens our spiritual connection, granting us clarity, peace, and an unwavering direction in our journey through life.

Brené Brown, a renowned researcher and storyteller, often speaks about vulnerability and its pivotal role in emotional well-being. She states, "Owning our story and loving ourselves through that process is the bravest thing we'll ever do."

When we own our thoughts, acknowledge our vulnerabilities, and navigate through them, we cultivate a healthy emotional environment that resonates with authenticity, compassion, and growth. In this space, distractions dissolve and our spiritual and emotional self thrives. This guides us towards a fulfilled and purposeful existence.

Tim Ferriss Leverages Social and Online Environment

Tim Ferriss is an entrepreneur, author, and podcaster best known for his book *The 4-Hour Workweek*, which explores concepts like "lifestyle design" and the "new rich," teaching people to be more intentional about their work-life balance and to create their own ideal environments.

Ferriss was not an overnight success. He tried different career paths and stumbled along the way, even facing severe burnout at one point. His first business venture in nutritional supplements was financially successful, but it left him feeling unfulfilled and overly stressed.

He knew that to make a real impact and enjoy his life, he had to be very intentional about his work and his environment. This inspired him to write *The 4-Hour Workweek*, which was initially rejected by twenty-six publishers before becoming a massive bestseller.

He used his blog to experiment with ideas and engage directly with his audience. His approach to A/B testing of headlines and subject matter gave him real-time feedback, allowing him to fine-tune his writing, online persona, and brand. He used social media strategically to promote himself and add value through sharing quality content and honest insights into his life and philosophies.

He then transitioned into podcasting. *The Tim Ferriss Show* was not just another marketing channel but a carefully curated environment where he could explore deep topics with experts in various fields. His preparation for each episode is rigorous; he often reads books from each guest and creates an environment where meaningful, transformative conversations can occur.

Today Tim Ferriss is not just an author or a podcaster. He's an influencer, effecting change in people's lives by encouraging them to be intentional about how they live, work, and interact. His success didn't come from merely creating content but from his thoughtfulness about what kind of content to create, how to engage with his audience, and how to continually adapt and grow.

Tim Ferriss's approach to leveraging social and online environments was methodical and reflective of his broader philosophy on life and work. Here's how he did it:

Experimentation and Engagement: Ferriss utilized his blog not just as a platform for sharing ideas, but as a laboratory for experimentation. By A/B testing different headlines and topics, he was able to gauge what resonated with his audience. This direct engagement provided invaluable feedback, allowing him to refine his content and tailor it to the interests and needs of his readers.

Strategic Use of Social Media: He didn't use social media as merely a promotional tool, but as a means to add value to his audience's lives. Ferriss shared quality content that was reflective of his life philosophies and insights, establishing a genuine connection with his followers. His strategic approach to social media helped in building his brand and expanding his reach.

Creating a Curated Podcast Environment: With *The Tim Ferriss Show*, he moved beyond conventional marketing strategies to create a platform for in-depth exploration of varied topics. Ferriss's meticulous preparation for each episode, including reading his guests' books and crafting thoughtful questions, ensured that the conversations were insightful and transformative. This wasn't just content creation; it was the cultivation of an environment conducive to learning and growth.

Intentionality and Adaptability: Ferriss's journey underscores the importance of being intentional about one's work and the environments one creates. His willingness to adapt, learn from feedback, and continually evolve his strategies were key to his success. This intentionality extended to every aspect of his brand, from the content of his blog and social media posts to the depth of his podcast discussions.

By thoughtfully engaging with his audience, experimenting with content, and creating a podcast that delivered substantial value, Ferriss was able to build a brand that resonated with a vast audience. His journey showcases the power of strategic online and social engagement for anyone looking to make an impact, be it in personal branding, launching a new project, or living a more intentional life.

Your Social and Digital Environment

Your social environment profoundly shapes your life's trajectory. The people you surround yourself with–family, friends, or colleagues–should be catalysts and cheerleaders for your personal growth and success. These individuals are your brain trust, offering constructive criticism, fresh perspectives, and invaluable wisdom.

Since we are shaped by the five people we spend the most time with, we might ask: Who are we around the most and how is their influence impacting our life?

Research supports the immense influence of our social circles on our well-being and success. One Harvard University study found that our chances of becoming obese rise by fifty-seven percent if a close friend becomes obese, illustrating the contagion effect of social circles on our behavior. Our happiness, health, and even how we think can ripple across our social networks.[iv]

So, surround yourself with positive power players, not naysayers. Ditch the drama queens and Negative Nellies. They're the brain fog you don't need. Get brave about weeding out folks who don't serve your vision. It might sting, but your future self will thank you.

Beyond your real-world social circles, you also have the universe in your pocket: your online environment. The digital realm is a double-edged sword. Emails, social media platforms, and online communities can either catapult you towards your goals or trap you in endless cycles of procrastination and comparison.

According to a LinkedIn study, professionals who engage meaningfully with their LinkedIn network are twenty-seven percent more likely to feel optimistic about their career growth and forty percent more likely to land a new gig. It's not just about racking up connections; it's about engaging with a network that aligns with your goals and aspirations.

Digital platforms can suck you into a vortex of time-wasting comparisons. The 2019 documentary *The Social Dilemma* highlighted the pitfalls of the addictive algorithms steering your behavior. Have you ever felt a pang of inadequacy as you scroll through curated success stories? You're not alone. This self-imposed "comparisonitis" is a toxic byproduct of a digitized life, and it's gnawing at your mental health.

Don't guilt-trip over that last Netflix binge or TikTok rabbit hole, but do audit your screen time. Your digital interactions should be as intentional as your live ones. It's like choosing between a nourishing meal and junk food. Both fill you up, but only one fuels you to perform. Theodore Roosevelt said it best: "Comparison is the great thief of joy."

Be a User, Not a Victim!

We know that social media can be addictive. In fact, in 2013, the Diagnostic and Statistical Manual of Mental Disorders (DSM-5-TR,) the official reference for mental health conditions, recognized Internet gambling as a true addiction. Hence, the spectrum of powerful reward triggers created by social media can be called not just a compulsion but a true addiction.

Given the allure of social media, how can you best navigate this digital ecosystem? By setting boundaries and applying intentionality both online and offline. A positive digital environment doesn't happen accidentally; you cultivate it. Think twice before hitting that "share" button or falling into a YouTube rabbit hole. Your future self will thank you.

Today your journey to success is not a solo expedition but a community trek, both online and offline. Choose your travel companions wisely. After all, the road to success is long and arduous; but with the right company, it can become the adventure of a lifetime.

Here are four ways to practice digital mindfulness.

Consume with intention. Mindless scrolling is the junk food of the digital age. Before you even unlock your phone, ask yourself: "Why am I here?" Are you seeking inspirational connections or merely looking to burn time? Self-awareness is your best weapon against digital gluttony. So, align your "clicks" with your intentions.

Limit your consumption. It's the twenty-first-century diet everyone needs: cutting down on screen time. Use apps and built-in phone settings to track your digital consumption. These tools are your calorie counters for screen time. When you get an alert saying you've been on Instagram for two hours, it's time to ease up. Log out several times a day to avoid any distractions.

Regularly do a digital detox. Allocate specific hours or entire days when you disconnect. This isn't just about avoiding a digital overdose; it's a hard reset for your brain. This gives your mind the space to recover, allowing you to bounce back with more focus and less mental fog.

***Engage in real life*!** Virtual likes are not as healthy as real laughter! Invest in face-to-face interactions. Revive an old hobby or dive into a new one. Rooting yourself in the real world yields immeasurable benefits, from stress reduction to cognitive development. Don't underestimate the magic of turning pages in a book or the adrenaline from a live soccer match.

When you get sucked into the vortex of someone else's online drama or perfectly curated life, ask yourself: Why does this content have a hold on you? Is it envy, aspiration, or just boredom? Identify the root cause and reroute that energy. If you get caught up in someone else's vacation photos, maybe it's time to plan an adventure of your own.

While the digital realm can be a space for inspiration, learning, and connection, it can also ensnare you in a web of comparison, distractions, and negativity–and leave you feeling hollow. It's up to you to navigate this space mindfully, ensuring that it serves your growth, well-being, and aspirations rather than detracting from them.

As you venture through the labyrinth of your goals and aspirations, your choices in curating your digital and physical environments are pivotal. Whether it's who you follow on social media or the podcasts you listen to, remember that you're not just a consumer–you are an architect of your environment.

Rob Dyrdek Reshapes His Environment

Speaking at an event alongside skateboarding icon and TV star Rob Dyrdek, I was struck by his compelling narrative, from the highs of his dynamic career and friendship with Christopher "Big Black" Boykin, which fueled the MTV hit *Rob & Big*, to the challenges that tested their bond and Dyrdek's career trajectory. Despite these trials, Dyrdek's disciplined daily routine played a crucial role in navigating through tumultuous times and reshaping his professional landscape.

Dyrdek's mornings, beginning between four a.m. and five a.m., are a testament to the discipline that underpins his approach to life and work. This early rise time, coupled with his practice of tracking daily metrics from body weight to mood, lays the foundation for a day focused on productivity and self-improvement. His commitment to "deep work" in the quiet early hours, followed by meditation in a high-tech pod, reflects a strategic approach to maintaining mental clarity amidst life's storms.

The physical discipline of an hour-long workout with a personal trainer and a structured meal plan underscores the importance Dyrdek places on physical health as part of his overall strategy to thrive in a challenging environment. This meticulous attention to wellness is not just about personal health but about creating an ecosystem where he can perform at his best.

When faced with the existential crisis of his friendship with Boykin and the dissonance in their professional world, Dyrdek's disciplined life approach extended to his decision to restructure his environment deliberately. Choosing to prioritize what mattered most, he meticulously rebuilt his professional ecosystem, making tough decisions to cut ties and focus on the future. This resolve led to the success of his venture studio, Dyrdek Machine, and the continued popularity of *Ridiculousness*, demonstrating how a disciplined daily routine can support significant life and career transformations.

Dyrdek's story, from navigating personal and professional upheavals to establishing a routine that champions discipline, health, and focused work, illustrates the power of one's environment as a strategic asset. It showcases that with the right daily practices and a willingness to reconfigure one's surroundings, overcoming even the most daunting obstacles is possible. In essence, Dyrdek's journey embodies the principle that it's not just about surviving challenges but about harnessing them to become a formidable force in one's own life.

Famous Marshmallow Experiment

Imagine yourself transported to the 1970s, a time when the field of psychology was on the cusp of a groundbreaking discovery. Dr. Walter Mischel, a pioneering researcher, found himself at the helm of an experiment that would reveal a profound insight into human psychology.

This experiment, known as the Stanford Marshmallow Experiment, may appear deceptively simple: a child, a room, and a marshmallow. However, its implications were all about creating an environment conducive to long-term success.

The participants in this intriguing experiment were young children between the ages of four and six. One by one, the children found themselves in a room and facing a tantalizing choice. In front of them was a single marshmallow. The challenge presented was straightforward: If the child could resist the temptation to eat the marshmallow for fifteen minutes, he or she would receive two marshmallows.

This test of delayed gratification revealed something far more profound–it could accurately predict future academic and professional achievements, offering a glimpse into the life trajectories of these participants. While many children succumbed to the allure of the marshmallow, some of the four- to six-year-olds demonstrated remarkable self-control. They had developed their own strategies to withstand the pull of instant gratification.

While the experiment focused on the children being able to exert self-control, it was also about their power of environmental control. These exceptional children were not simply relying on sheer willpower. Instead, they became architects of their immediate surroundings, crafting an environment aligned with their long-term aspirations. Some sang songs; others engaged in self-talk; and a few simply averted their gaze. One even took a nap. They were proactive participants in their own destiny, taking control of their environment to shape their future.

Let me repeat that.

While the experiment focused on the children being able to exert self-control, it was also about their power of environmental control. These exceptional children were not simply relying on sheer willpower. Instead, they became architects of their immediate surroundings, crafting an environment aligned with their long-term aspirations. Some sang songs; others engaged in self-talk; and a few simply averted their gaze. One even took a nap. They were proactive participants in their own destiny, taking control of their environment to shape their future.

As years passed, Dr. Mischel's follow-up studies revealed a remarkable transformation among these children. Those who had successfully conquered the marshmallow test outperformed their peers in astonishing ways. On average, they scored 210 points higher on SATs, enjoyed better health, achieved higher incomes, and cultivated more fulfilling relationships. Mischel's research uncovered a profound connection between the ability to delay gratification and achieve real-world success, even accurately predicting academic achievements years in advance.

Mastering Your Environment

Mastering your environment doesn't guarantee success, but it tips the odds in your favor. Whether you're facing the temptation of a marshmallow or tackling a complex project, strategically shaping your surroundings can provide an advantage. It's not about seizing the instant reward, but setting the stage for a lifetime of achievement. When you design your environment, you gain a powerful influence over the outcome.

The skill to set and maintain boundaries is a major component of Mastering Minimums. This was a hard-earned lesson for me as a recovering people pleaser. The urge to be liked led me to make decisions that were not in my best interest. When you attempt to please everyone, you end up pleasing fewer people.

When I learned to establish *loving boundaries*, my environment transformed into a more nurturing space that respected my well-being. You might think of setting boundaries as putting distance between you and others and pushing people away. However, a loving boundary is the exact opposite. It draws certain lines in the sand where you tell people, "This is how I want to be treated in this space."

Establishing boundaries is a self-care strategy. While some relationships can complicate this process, you must take the initiative because no one else will do it. You can lovingly tell people what's acceptable and it's okay if they have a differing opinion. It's about respecting your choices and knowing you are doing what is best for you and your vision.

Remember that maintaining boundaries is an ongoing process, not a one-time task. If you don't stick to your boundaries consistently, you're merely making requests and not setting boundaries. The responsibility to enforce these boundaries falls on your shoulders.

For me, setting loving boundaries meant prioritizing my mental and emotional well-being. I had friends who I deeply cared for, and yet I recognized that their presence wasn't helping my personal growth. So, I established a loving boundary. They would occasionally be my friends for group activities but would no longer be part of my regular circle.

This decision wasn't about them. It was about my commitment to create an environment that served my growth. I love people! I love people to be themselves! I also know that some people are being themselves and don't support me, which is okay. It's my job to decide with whom I spend my time.

SECTION 3

SUSTAIN SUCCESS

Action 7: Defeat Demons with Discipline

"With self-discipline, most anything is possible."

– Theodore Roosevelt

"Fairy tales are more than true: not because they tell us that we exist, but because they tell us that we can be beaten."

– Neil Gaiman

Discipline keeps us focused, accountable, and consistent. With discipline we can overcome personal demons like self-doubt, fear, limiting beliefs, and professional setbacks. When we embark on the path to success, formidable obstacles, challenges, and unexpected threats emerge. These "demons" come not only from the outside but from inside yourself. Your inner and outer demons want to tear down your castle, posing a threat to everything you've painstakingly built.

By taking Minimum or Standards actions daily, you establish a protective shield against distractions and demons. Instead of getting bogged down by the complexity and magnitude of a task, you can zone in on the simple, actionable steps. You reclaim your agency. You control your time, energy, and focus. Your resilience strengthens your resolve and trains your mind to discern between the essentials and the distractions.

If discipline feels challenging, revisit your vision, reignite your commitment, review your actions, and check your mindset. Remain steadfast in your commitment to your aspirations, ready to make sacrifices and trade-offs along the way.

Internal and External Demons and Distractions

Inner and outer demons pose a serious threat to your castle!

Internal demons live inside you, inside your castle. They arise from our own thoughts, emotions, beliefs, or habits. They might manifest as self-doubt, anxiety, procrastination, or low motivation.

Your job is to identify them and get rid of them. If you can't do it on your own, seek professional, spiritual or medical help. These internal demons can be difficult to exterminate because they're part of you, perhaps originating in your childhood. They may try to deceive you, and tell you that you can't win; make you overconfident; try to distract you from your goals; or urge you to drink too much or to cheat on your spouse.

With effort and focus, over time you can chase away these demons so they don't impede your progress. But it takes vigilance, because they always try to sneak back in! Internal demons lie within your power to overcome. You may need to shift mindset, develop new habits, seek guidance from coaches or therapists, and practice self-reflection and self-awareness.

External demons arise from factors beyond our control–other people, circumstances, or events. While they are not always in your control, you can anticipate them and defend against distractions and forces of destruction. These demons circle around your castle like bats, flapping their wings and seeking to thwart your efforts. Alas, in today's world, distractions and demons lurk in every corner. From the incessant beeping of mobile notifications to the seemingly urgent matters that demand our attention, these diversions can subtly sabotage our goals. Such challenges can often make us overlook simple solutions.

If we allow distractions and demons to dominate our life, our days would turn into weeks and weeks would turn into months without achievements. We would constantly react to events, chasing after the next shiny thing instead of proactively charting our path. This perpetual reaction and distraction cycle erodes our self-confidence and clouds our vision. Ultimately, our potential would become a shadow of what it could have been and the dreams we once held dear would seem out of reach.

Many people today are literally driving distracted. I reminded my daughter that she would be distracted if music blared while she was on her phone. I explained that, as the driver, she can control most distractions. She can turn down the music. By law, she *must* put her phone away and limit the number of passengers. Likewise, we all have the power to limit our distractions.

Distractions and demons often disguise themselves as urgent matters, luring us into sidelining our core priorities. The world screams, "Go big or go home!" We're flooded with notions that unless we take massive action, we're making no progress. There's social media buzz, the allure of "the next big thing," or the pressure to always be in "hustle mode."

We often consider small, consistent efforts as insignificant. But in reality our Minimums, in their deceptive simplicity, are the unsung heroes of sustained success. A marathon isn't won in a sprint, but with consistent pacing; and progress in life isn't always about giant leaps, but consistent small steps.

Name and Shame Those Demons!

Both inner and outer demons conspire to push you back and bring you down. Don't let them. Keep vigilant and keep them out of your castle and your life! You need to identify the inner and outer demons trying to sabotage your castle. Your progress depends not only on your positive energy, but on how many demons you can remove from your castle.

Identifying your inner demons can be a painful exercise.
Do you drink too much alcohol or eat too much junk food? Are you impatient with others, or judgmental? Are you easily distracted by social media or other entertainments? Do you spend all your money instead of saving some?

Preparation can prevent demons from wreaking their havoc. If you are building your castle near the seashore, you build it high enough–even using stilts–to keep it safe from rising waters! You might buy fire insurance or a home security system. You might anticipate future home values, or check out neighborhood schools. You make sure that the city has a professional police department. And you would use quality materials to build your castle.

Your Minimums might include doing the necessary repairs to your castle and keeping it clean and free of pests such as mice or termites. Your Minimums not only serve to advance your progress, they are also necessary to *maintain* your castle.

Steve Jobs Faces His Demons

Steve Jobs, the visionary co-founder of Apple who navigated treacherous waters, faced his share of relentless demons. In 1985, Jobs found himself ousted from the company he helped create. The demons of corporate politics and power struggles had triumphed, and they threw him out!

Here is where the hero's journey takes an intriguing twist. Instead of succumbing to despair, Jobs viewed this unexpected setback as an opportunity for growth and transformation. Undeterred, he founded a new venture called NeXT and it was a company that would catalyze innovation in computing.

Like a hero returning from exile, Jobs acquired a struggling animation studio which would become Pixar. Under his leadership, Pixar produced beloved classics including *Toy Story* and *Finding Nemo* which solidified its place in cinematic history.

Then, in a triumphant return, Jobs returned with renewed vigor to Apple: the company he co-founded. He brought with him a new vision that would redefine the technology industry. Introducing groundbreaking products like the iPhone and the iPad transformed Apple and the tech landscape.

Steve Jobs had faced his demons, the moment of exile and uncertainty, and emerged renewed and resolute. He was not scorched or defeated. His journey exemplifies the resilience and transformative power that can arise from confronting life's fiercest challenges.

Lessons for us. Like Jobs, who saw his ousting from Apple not as an end but as a new beginning, we can transform our demons from destructive beasts into empowering allies.

Even the most disciplined and focused individuals have their demons and encounter obstacles and setbacks to success. The key lies in recognizing these challenges early and devising strategies to conquer them. Facing challenges doesn't require being fearless or invincible. It's about summoning courage, persisting in adversity, and learning from challenges and setbacks. Steve Jobs exemplified this by turning setbacks into opportunities.

By identifying your demons, you gain insight into your strengths and weaknesses. This enables you to confront future obstacles. Armed with the right mindset, tools, and strategies, you can conquer any obstacle that arises and emerge stronger and more triumphant.

The road to success is seldom straight. It's filled with twists, turns, and challenges. These are not your enemies–they are teachers in disguise, showing you where you can grow stronger, more resilient, and more aligned with your purpose.

Lincoln: Unveiling Your Path to Victory

Abraham Lincoln, the sixteenth president of the United States, faced a demon like no other: the American Civil War. Torn between the weight of his office and the unimaginable scale of human suffering, he had to navigate a fractured nation. More than 600,000 lives hung in the balance as brother fought against brother.

Lincoln's primary distraction wasn't just the battlefield but the splinters within his own cabinet and the rampant criticism from the press. A lesser leader might've capitulated and sought the easier path of appeasement, but not Lincoln.

His agonizing decision to issue the Emancipation Proclamation in 1863 was the turning point. It wasn't just about ending slavery; it was a strategic masterpiece that reframed the war as a fight for human freedom. It galvanized the North, crippled the Confederacy's hopes for foreign aid, and paved the way for African Americans to serve in the Union forces–over 180,000 enlisted.

The Union won the war in 1865, slavery was abolished, and Lincoln's leadership through the Thirteenth Amendment changed the DNA of the nation. Under his leadership, the United States became a symbol of a united–rather than a divided–land. His Gettysburg Address, just 271 words long, redefined the American ideal.

That's the thing about demons. They are big and terrifying, but they often guard treasure. For Lincoln, the treasure was a united nation built on the principles of freedom and equality. It's a legacy that still resonates, along with this compelling lesson: Your most ferocious demons hide your most significant rewards, even your own legacy.

We must recognize and confront our internal demons–the fears, doubts, and negative self-talk that hinder our progress and happiness. They can be incredibly challenging because they often remain hidden from others and from us.

For example: Suppose that someone has an internal demon of "fear of failure." This fear may prevent them from taking risks or pursuing their aspirations, as they fear falling short or being criticized. To combat this demon, they may need to challenge their negative self-talk and replace it with ***positive affirmations***, such as, "I am capable of achieving my aspirations," or "I am resilient and can bounce back from setbacks." They also need to take Minimum actions towards their aspirations, gradually building their confidence and overcoming their fears.

Sylvester Stallone: Rocky Start

In the late 1970s, **Sylvester Stallone** was at the lowest point in his career. His speech impediment made it difficult for him to land roles and he was broke, barely making ends meet. He faced relentless doubt, both from within and from the industry. He worked as a cleaner at a zoo and was occasionally homeless, sleeping in the Port Authority Bus Terminal. He was so financially desperate that he sold his dog, Butkus, for $50 to keep the lights on.

Despite countless rejections and setbacks, Stallone had a burning desire to become an actor and screenwriter. He knew he had talent, but since so many saw no potential in him it was a battle against self-doubt.

The turning point came when Stallone decided to write his own script, a story about an underdog boxer named Rocky Balboa. He believed in this project wholeheartedly, and despite facing rejection after rejection he refused to compromise on his vision.

His screenplay for *Rocky* was his shot at redemption. He pitched it to producers, but they wanted a proven star to lead. They offered $360,000 for the script, but with one catch–Stallone wouldn't star in it. That was the raging storm: accept the money, lose his dream role, or stick with an uncertain future.

Standing his ground, Stallone refused the lucrative deal. He wanted to be Rocky, to bring to life the underdog he knew so well. The studio finally relented, offering him a paltry $20,000 and a percentage of the film's profits but allowing him to star. With unyielding resolve, he poured every fiber of his being into the role. He even insisted on doing his own stunts to lend authenticity.

The clouds broke. *Rocky* grossed $225 million worldwide against a $1 million budget and bagged three Academy Awards, including Best Picture. More than just accolades, the movie spawned a franchise with eight films that collectively raked in over $1.7 billion. Stallone bought back his dog for $15,000 and a role in the movie, a testament to full-circle redemption.

Beyond *Rocky* he conquered another franchise, *Rambo*, pushing his lifetime box office tally to an astonishing $727 million. Stallone didn't just survive the storm; he became the master of it.

In the face of monumental choices and relentless trials, fortified by his own self-belief, Stallone chose to battle his external and internal demons. The rest is not just Hollywood history but a lesson in enduring the tempests of life with grit and audacity. Stallone's legacy is not just in his movies but in the inspiration he provides for anyone striving to turn their dreams into reality.

Facing the Demon of Self-Doubt

We need defenses against self-doubt. Some of these defenses include self-affirmations, positive experiences, and our unshakable belief in our strengths. These defenses enable us to navigate challenging times, recognizing that each obstacle presents an opportunity for growth.

To face the demon of doubt head-on means to recognize its presence and arm ourselves with the weapons of self-belief, perseverance, and positive reinforcement. It means surrounding ourselves with people who believe in our vision, even when it is hard to see it ourselves. Every word of encouragement, every gesture of support, strengthens the defense of our castle.

Regularly reconnect with your passion and purpose, reminding yourself of your "why." This acts as a beacon of light during the darkest moments of doubt, guiding you through the storm.

Doubt, like any other emotion, is natural. The goal isn't to eradicate doubt but to ensure it doesn't gain a stronghold. Embracing the presence of doubt and addressing it openly means depriving it of its power over us. We can tame this demon of self-doubt lurking in the shadows by seeking counsel, engaging in self-reflection, and persistently revisiting our vision.

Wrestling External Demons

External demons are an inevitable part of life. By addressing challenges such as financial stress, work-related issues, relationship problems, health concerns, and societal pressures, we can develop strategies to manage and overcome them. This process builds resilience, empowers us, and creates a more fulfilling life.

Financial stress is a common external challenge. It can result from student loans, credit card debts, unemployment, or struggles to cover basic expenses. We may unknowingly create our own financial demons through poor spending habits and living beyond our means. Thus, some people deal with the financial demon their entire lives.

We must recognize how our choices sometimes contribute to these demons. For example: I know someone who loved buying designer clothes. Her demon was her drive for materialism to fill a void in her life. Since she couldn't afford designer clothes she resorted to using credit cards, experiencing a temporary high with each shopping spree but ultimately succumbing to defeat and debt when the bills arrived.

Her designer demon led her to bankruptcy. Even during the moments of high, wearing her designer things, she was still stuck in this desperation that no handbag could save her from. After her devastating bankruptcy, she got help and saw what was missing in her life. It wasn't until she felt utterly defeated by this demon that she learned how to conquer it.

Addressing financial stress requires creating a practical budget, prioritizing debt repayment, seeking professional advice when necessary, and adopting a mindset of gratitude while focusing on non-material aspects of life.

We must also acknowledge the dangers of substance abuse and overconsumption of drugs, alcohol, video games, excessive screen time, and pornography. These addictions can have devastating impacts on our physical and mental well-being, strain relationships, and lead to financial struggles.

Some demons may appear once and never return. For example: As a teenager I decided to never drink alcohol, defeating that demon once and for all. However, for others, demons can become lifelong nemeses that lurk outside their castle walls and are ready to strike at any moment.

One of my friends is a recovering drug user. Every day he wakes up knowing that the drug demon is waiting, patiently looking for a moment of weakness to strike. He has been sober for over three decades and yet he faces this demon daily, affirming that today will *not* be the day it wins. These pesky demons can appear periodically or daily, testing our resolve and strength.

Mental and Physical Distractions

Mental and physical distractions can derail even our most determined goals. For many of us, the most potent distraction is our mindset. Our brains are hardwired to find the path of least resistance and craft narratives that support staying within our comfort zone. The myriad distractions around us constantly shift our focus from our pure desires.

One distraction could be the endless influx of information, the perpetual cycle of breaking news, or the seemingly innocent ping of a notification. Each distraction chips away at our resolve.

The demon of distraction is subtle and insidious. Its nature makes it difficult to detect until it's already diverted our path. Distractions are such formidable foes because they are intertwined with our human nature. Our minds are curious, and new stimuli seek our attention in our fast-paced, interconnected world. This environment is the perfect breeding ground for distraction.

External distractions are often the most noticeable. They are interruptions from our surroundings, like a ringing phone, a colleague's question, or a sudden, appealing thought about what's for dinner. These distractions appear trivial, but cumulatively they profoundly impact our focus and progress. Developing an environment that minimizes disruptions becomes crucial, as does setting clear boundaries with those around us and crafting spaces where we can concentrate.

Elusive internal distractions can be even more disruptive. These originate within our own minds. These thoughts can quickly derail our focus, whether it's a nagging doubt, a tantalizing daydream, or an unchecked desire to look in on social media.

Overcoming internal distractions requires self-understanding. Mindfulness practices play a pivotal role, helping us become more attuned to our mental state and enabling us to guide our focus back when it begins to waver.

Distractions disguised as necessities can be the most deceptive of all. Sometimes we find ourselves caught up in activities that feel productive but take us away from our core objectives. Whether it's excessive planning, constant learning without application, or engaging in tasks that don't align with our goals, these disguised distractions can lead us astray. Recognizing and combating them requires a clear understanding of our goals and constant vigilance to ensure our actions align with our aspirations.

Facing and conquering the distraction demon is not about building an impenetrable fortress where no distraction can enter. That's impossible! It's about cultivating the wisdom to recognize when we're being pulled away from our path and the strength to guide ourselves back. It's a dance that requires grace, understanding, and persistence.

While external and internal demons are inevitable, we are not powerless in their presence. Through our daily actions and commitment to Minimum, Standard, and Blitz actions, we fortify ourselves against these demons. We develop habits, discipline, and a winning mindset that enable us to face challenges head-on, even in adversity. Over time we become stronger, more resilient, and capable of withstanding any storm that comes our way.

Your Inner Compass

Since demons and distractions try to confuse you and throw you off course, in order to stay true to your vision and values you need a strong ***inner compass***–a set of guiding principles deeply ingrained within you. These principles are like the North Star, a constant reference point that helps you find your way, especially during uncertainty and doubt when the demons are making their mischief and clouding your vision with fog.

Our inner compass–consisting of our core values, beliefs, passions, principles and convictions that define who we are and what we stand for–ensures that we stay on the right path, even when we can't see it clearly. When you feel lost in the fog, when external circumstances or self-doubt threatens to divert you from your path, your inner compass points you towards your true north, your ultimate destination. It keeps you focused on your Minimum and Standard actions, and helps you prepare for the occasional Blitz that will change your life.

You can navigate through any fog by relying on your inner compass and holding fast to your priorities–your dreams and aspirations. Your inner compass is your anchor, providing direction and purpose even when the journey becomes challenging. Every journey has risks, obstacles, temptations, and distractions; however, your inner compass can guide you through the fog, helping you make choices aligned with your values and long-term goals. So, carry your inner compass with you always. It will be your steadfast guide, ensuring that you stay true to your values and stay on course towards fulfilling your dreams.

It's a tragic tale that unfolds time and time again: A person achieves success and begins to bask in their accomplishments. They start mingling with individuals who don't align with their values. Their environment shifts as they adopt the mindset of "I'm successful now." They gradually drift away from their true self. They lose focus on their priorities. They become complacent, overconfident, and neglect mastering the fundamentals.

Tiger: Into and Out of the Woods

In 2009, champion golfer **Tiger Woods** faced a public and personal crisis. As the public learned of multiple infidelities, he faced media scrutiny and his personal life unraveled. While some sponsors like Nike stood by him, others like AT&T and Accenture severed ties.

Though battered and damaged, his castle remained intact. Then came another brutal hit: his game deteriorated. In 2014, for the first time, he dropped out of the top 100 World Golf Rankings. It wasn't just a fall from grace but a freefall into an abyss.

But instead of continuing the nosedive, Woods retreated–not in defeat, but to rebuild from scratch. In a bold Blitz action, he fired his coach, caddie, and entourage. Then he faced his most formidable opponent yet: himself. Woods went through rigorous physical and mental training. He even underwent spinal fusion surgery, which took him out of the game for nearly a year.

The result? His 2019 Master's win was his first major championship in eleven years and his fifteenth major title overall. Statistically, Woods went from being outside the top one thousand in World Golf Rankings in 2017 to reclaim a spot in the top ten by 2019. According to *Forbes*, his estimated earnings were $64 million that same year.

Woods saw disaster looming. External and internal demons were circling and clawing at him. In response he took a massive Blitz action, demolished his castle of arrogance and entitlement, and built a fortress of humility and grit. Now the crowd roars for the athlete and for the man who walked away from the wrong path, found his compass, and reclaimed his kingdom.

Lessons for us: At specific points in our lives, we all wander away from ourselves. We often engage in actions against our identity for various reasons. Sometimes we venture out into unfamiliar territory without facing immediate consequences. We have to remember: There will be consequences! We can't walk away from our true selves without experiencing repercussions.

Straying from Your Core Values

Your true path represents the choices and actions that align with your values and principles. Straying from your path is like venturing into unknown territories without armor, map, or compass. As you walk away from your path, the route becomes less clear, more rugged, and fraught with obstacles. The farther you stray, the more difficult it becomes to find your way back to your true self. In your confused state, your demons see a chance to attack.

Venturing from your true path can be seen as a shortcut or an easy way out, but every step taken from your path makes it harder to find your way back. When we walk away from our true path, we become vulnerable to external influences, pressures, and temptations that can lead us astray. The tragedy of straying from our true path isn't just about the potential missteps or pitfalls. It's also about the time and opportunities lost, the energy expended on paths that don't serve our purpose, and the erosion of the identity and values that define us.

The good news is that it's never too late to turn around. The path back might be arduous, requiring atonement. Yet with every step we take towards our true path, we reaffirm our commitment to our true selves and core values. Also, our return journey to our true path can provide invaluable lessons. These experiences refine our character, teaching us resilience, understanding, and the cost of abandoning our values. They remind us why we chose our true path in the first place and inspire us to fortify our commitment.

When you face a crossroads, ask yourself: "Is this step taking me closer to or father away from my true path? Am I listening to my heart or to demons urging me to go the wrong way?" By choosing the path that aligns with your values and vision, you stay true to yourself.

Resilience in the Face of Adversity

Storms, trials, duress, hard times, and tragedy test our discipline. Sometimes the demons win and we act against our values, betray our true selves, and abandon our true path.

For instance: Consider the TV show *Shrinking*. The opening scene sets the stage with Jason Segel as therapist Jimmy Laird in a state of moral collapse. Picture him floating aimlessly in his pool, cocktail in hand, as anonymous women linger. It's a tableau of excess and emptiness.

He's estranged from his daughter, who can't reconcile this hollow man with the father she once knew. Then, as the episode unfolds, we learn the catalyst: the sudden loss of his wife. The tragedy shook Laird to his core, sending him spiraling away from his priorities and values into a self-destructive free-fall.

To save himself from his inner demons, he begins intervening in the lives of his patients so they can expedite the changes they desire. This is a piercing look at how life's calamities can uproot us from our core beliefs.

We all know people who abandon their priorities after experiencing a tragic event, such as receiving news of a loved one's life-threatening illness or death. In such times, overwhelming emotions like grief, fear, and sadness can drive people to act in ways that contradict their values and priorities. Some may turn to unhealthy coping mechanisms like substance abuse, overeating, or self-harm. Others may withdraw from their loved ones and seek solitude, prioritizing their need for privacy over social connection and support.

To navigate these situations, we may need to seek support and guidance from trusted sources such as family members, friends, or mental health professionals. By reaching out for help we can better manage our emotions and behaviors, prioritize our values, heal, and recover.

When we make mistakes and act against our values, we may experience embarrassment, shame, or guilt. Naming and shaming our demons–and taking responsibility for our actions–is a step towards reclaiming our true selves and regaining our sense of identity. This may involve apologizing to those affected by our behavior and taking other steps to make amends.

Introspection and self-reflection are potent tools for reconnecting with our values after acting in ways that contradict them. We can prevent similar situations by examining our behavior, identifying the factors that led us astray, and making necessary changes. This may involve setting new boundaries or prioritizing our values when making decisions.

Consider the example of partners who cheat in a relationship, contradicting their values and commitment to their family. Their action does not define them entirely. They remain the same person they were before, with the same vision and priorities. While they may have faced a monster and lost, it doesn't mean they must burn down the castle.

By reconnecting with their vision and values they can begin to move forward, make amends for their actions, and rebuild their castle. This may involve seeking forgiveness, attending counseling to address underlying issues, and renewing their commitment to family and values. Sometimes the damage is too significant to salvage the relationship, but the work to improve the castle still must be done regardless of the immediate outcome.

During a recovery process, we must show ourselves compassion and avoid harsh self-judgment. We're all human and we all make mistakes. We can move forward with greater clarity and purpose by acknowledging our faults and taking steps to address them.

When confronted with external or internal demons, giving up or losing sight of our vision and values may be tempting. However, by reconnecting with ourselves and our aspirations we can weather any battle and emerge stronger on the other side. Remember to have compassion for yourself and remain committed to your castle and vision, no matter what challenges may arise.

We Can Choose How We React

I know firsthand the pain and challenge of confronting life's harshest realities. Losing my brother Danny was a profoundly personal and agonizing ordeal. Such experiences can shake one's foundation. In the face of profound loss, our values are truly tested.

While we cannot control the tragedies that happen to us or the external demons that attack us, ***we can choose how we react to them***. Do we allow our grief to pull us into a downward spiral, abandoning our castle and all that we hold dear? Or do we harness that pain, channel it into strength, and use it to fortify our castle walls, moat, and drawbridge?

Danny's loss could have been a reason for me to walk away from my castle, abandon my values, and give in to despair. But I chose to honor Danny's memory by clinging tight to my values, by not letting grief dictate my actions, and by using the pain to remain true to myself.

We all face challenges–personal losses, betrayals, professional setbacks. We have a choice in how we respond. We can let these monsters burn down our castle or we can stand firm, draw from our reservoirs of strength, and confront these challenges head-on. When we do, we protect our castle and make it more formidable than ever.

In our darkest moments, we need to remember our vision, our values, and why we built our castle in the first place. These guiding lights can lead us back when we stray, give us the strength to face our demons, and inspire us to rebuild even when all seems lost. Our castle then becomes a reflection of our indomitable spirit and our unyielding commitment to our true selves.

Weathering Storms

Sustaining our personal castle is about weathering storms. Even in our darkest moments, we can reinforce the walls of our fortress rather than abandon it. Storms are inevitable and the forecast often changes without warning. Our proactive actions fortify us, enabling us to remain grounded and focused during tumultuous times when demons attack with the fury of a storm.

Taking shelter from storms, chaos, and uncertainty requires turning inward and prioritizing what truly matters. It entails focusing on our vision, priorities, and environments and taking deliberate actions. Sheltering from the storm also cultivates inner strength and resilience. It places trust in our abilities and instincts. This can empower us to confront any challenge.

Maintaining a robust support system is equally essential during challenging times. This network can comprise friends, family, mentors, or professional counselors who provide guidance, encouragement, and emotional support. Just as a castle has guards and knights to ward off external threats, we can rely on our support system to help navigate the trials of life.

Storms are transitory and will eventually pass. Although the light at the end of the tunnel may seem dim during difficult moments, retaining hope and trust in a brighter future is crucial. By remaining committed to our vision, prioritizing self-care, and relying on our support system, we can weather life's storms and emerge more substantial and resilient.

Madam Walker: Summoning the Guardian Within

The Netflix series *Self Made: Inspired by the Life of* **Madam C.J. Walker** reveals a journey marked by significant challenges and extraordinary success. Born into the depths of poverty in a world dominated by male entrepreneurs, Walker stood as a Black woman defiant against societal odds. Her vision was bold: to empower Black women through specialized hair care products.

She faced financial destitution, skepticism from a doubting public, and a personal health crisis–a scalp disorder causing hair loss. With incredible willpower, Madam Walker rose to meet these challenges. Her response was a blend of innovation and sheer determination. She developed a unique haircare treatment tailored for Black women. This breakthrough marked a pivotal moment in her story: adversity transformed into opportunity.

With an initial investment of only $1.25, Walker began manufacturing her product. She reached out to historically marginalized and overlooked communities, selling a product and a promise of empowerment. As her business grew she trained over twenty thousand women as sales agents and entrepreneurs, fostering a spirit of independence and financial autonomy.

Walker's business acumen led to extraordinary success. She became the first self-made female millionaire in America, with her company generating $500,000 annually by 1919 (more than $7 million in today's currency.) Her success was not just in her wealth but in her ability to break barriers and redefine the landscape for Black women in business.

And she built herself a castle! In 1917 Walker commissioned Vertner Tandy, the first licensed Black architect in New York City, to design a magnificent house in Irvington-on-Hudson, New York. She called it Villa Lewaro. It cost $250,000 to build ($4.6 million today) and was lavishly furnished. She made it a gathering place for community leaders and to inspire other African Americans to pursue their dreams.

She moved into the house in May 1918 and hosted an opening event to honor Emmett Jay Scott, at that time the Assistant Secretary for Negro Affairs of the U.S. Department of War. The house is still there. It became a National Historic Landmark in 1976 and has been a private residence since the mid-1980s.

Madam C. J. Walker's story, as portrayed in *Self Made*, is a powerful example of resilience and vision. Faced with powerful demons, she turned her struggles into catalysts for monumental achievement. Her legacy proves that with determination and strategic action, even the most difficult obstacles can be transformed into pathways for extraordinary success.

Lesson for Us: when the demons come–and they will–we need to safeguard our progress and priorities. Life inevitably presents challenges that threaten to derail our progress or divert us from our chosen path. We face moments of uncertainty, succumb to external pressures, or endure the tumultuous storms of life's trials. Yet maintaining our focus on progress and priorities becomes crucial during these times.

Cultivating Resilience to Overcome Setbacks

Obstacles and setbacks are inevitable parts of life's journey and play a big role in our growth and development. When faced with challenges, we need to recognize that they provide valuable feedback and opportunities for learning. They allow us to reflect on our strategies, identify areas for improvement, and gain insights that can propel us forward.

Getting knocked down by setbacks is part of the process. It's okay to take a moment to lick our wounds and regroup. In these moments of adversity, our resilience is tested. Our ability to get back up, dust ourselves off, and continue moving forward becomes the defining factor in our success.

> *"Don't wish it were easier. Wish you were better."*
>
> *– Jim Rohn*

Having the right mindset is crucial when facing obstacles and setbacks. Adopting a growth mindset allows us to view challenges as opportunities for development. Instead of being discouraged, we can see setbacks as stepping stones to future success. As Jim Rohn wisely advised, "Don't wish it were easier, wish you were better." This mindset shift empowers us to approach setbacks with a solution-oriented mindset, seeking lessons and adjustments to strengthen our future endeavors.

Setbacks provide us with valuable insights and feedback. They illuminate areas where we may need to improve our skills, strategies, or approaches. By embracing these moments as learning opportunities, we can refine our methods and develop resilience.

Setbacks and obstacles are integral parts of our journey. They test our determination and provide contrast for us to appreciate the sweet taste of success. Embracing setbacks as valuable learning experiences help us grow stronger and wiser–to rise from the fall, persist despite the obstacles, and maintain a positive, growth-oriented mindset.

Setbacks are temporary and we can overcome them. With resilience, determination, and a willingness to learn, we can use setbacks as stepping stones to achieve our goals and create a more fulfilling and meaningful life.

When you embark on any transformative journey, seek to emulate champions like Madam C.J. Walker and Sylvester Stallone. Their tales echo the spirit of perseverance and discipline.

Self vs Situation: Reclaiming Your Vision

The **Stanford Prison Experiment**, led by psychologist Philip Zimbardo in 1971, is a profound example of how situations can dramatically influence human behavior and often lead people to act in ways that contradict their standards, values, and priorities. This experiment, involving twenty-four male college students in a mock prison setting, was designed to explore the psychological effects of perceived power and imprisonment.

Male students were recruited from the local community and paid fifteen dollars per day to participate in a "psychological study of prison life." Volunteers were randomly assigned to be prisoners or prison guards. During the study, held in the basement of Stanford University's psychology building, the volunteers selected to be guards were given uniforms designed to de-individuate them and they were instructed to prevent prisoners from escaping.

This study's most startling outcome was the participants' rapid and intense behavior transformation. The guards, who were ordinary students with no prior indications of sadistic tendencies, quickly adopted authoritarian and abusive behaviors. This shift was unexpected and alarming, considering these individuals were pre-screened for psychological stability and showed no predisposition for such extreme behavior.

Within a few days, the guards began to employ psychological tactics like humiliation and intimidation. Their actions escalated to physical punishment and food deprivation. This behavior was not instructed or encouraged by the study's design; it emerged spontaneously from the power dynamics of the prison environment.

On the other side, the prisoners, also ordinary students, began to exhibit signs of extreme stress, passivity, and submissiveness. Their identities started to dissolve into their assigned roles, with some even referring to themselves by their prisoner numbers instead of their names.

The experiment, initially planned for two weeks, was terminated after six days due to the ethical concerns raised by the participants' behavior and the structure of the experiment itself. After the study about twenty percent of the participants sought psychological counseling, highlighting the profound impact of the experiment on their mental health.

Despite its scientific flaws, the Stanford Prison Experiment revealed that under certain conditions, especially those involving power dynamics and role-playing, we can rapidly and profoundly deviate from our personal values and ethical standards. It underscores the importance of being aware of situational influences and safeguarding our values and priorities. While we may have a strong sense of self and a clear set of values, we are also susceptible to the influence of our environment and our roles, since challenging circumstances can impact our behavior as we strive to uphold our standards and values.

The Hero's Journey

In many ways, you are the hero of your own story, in which you end with many memories and few unfulfilled dreams. And at your core is the virtue of discipline.

In literature, the hero's journey serves as a framework for many narratives across various cultures and genres. It was first articulated by the mythologist and writer Joseph Campbell in his 1949 book *The Hero with a Thousand Faces*. This concept describes a common pattern that protagonists undergo in their quests and adventures, transcending cultural boundaries and time periods.

The hero's journey comprises ten stages:

1. ***Call to adventure.*** The hero is presented with a challenge, a problem, or a call to action that disrupts the hero's ordinary world and sets him or her on a path of transformation.

2. ***Refusal of the call.*** Initially, the hero may resist the call due to fear, doubt, or a desire to stay in their comfort zone. This reluctance adds depth to their character.

3. ***Crossing the threshold.*** Eventually, the hero decides to embark on the journey, leaving behind the familiar and venturing into the unknown to deal with change and self-discovery.

4. ***Trials and challenges.*** Along the way, the hero faces a series of tests, obstacles, and adversaries. These trials foster character development and the acquisition of skills or knowledge.

5. ***Meeting allies and mentors.*** The hero often encounters allies and mentors who provide guidance, support, and wisdom. These characters help the hero navigate the challenges.

6. ***Ordeal.*** At this critical moment in the hero's journey, they face their most significant challenge or confrontation. It's a make-or-break point that leads to a profound transformation.

7. ***Reward.*** After overcoming the ordeal, the hero reaps the rewards, both tangible (treasure or recognition) and intangible (self-discovery or enlightenment.)

8. ***The Road Back.*** The hero decides to return to their ordinary world, carrying the wisdom and power gained during the journey. This return may pose new challenges or require sacrifices.

9. ***Resurrection.*** In the final confrontation, the hero faces a climactic battle or challenge that solidifies their transformation and reinforces their growth.

10. ***Return with the elixir.*** The hero returns to their ordinary world, sharing the wisdom or rewards they gained during their journey. This benefits both the hero and the community.

In the crucible of adversity, ***discipline*** becomes our staunchest ally. It is the thread that weaves the tapestry of success, the anchor that keeps us steadfast in the face of adversity.

McRaven: A Showcase of Discipline's Might

The life of Admiral William H. McRaven is a testament to the power of discipline. He is a highly respected retired United States Navy SEAL who is renowned for his leadership in the military, including overseeing the successful operation to capture Osama bin Laden in 2011.

But in the summer of 2001, his career–and almost his life–nearly came to an end. During a routine parachute training exercise in San Diego, while in the midst of a freefall, a fellow skydiver prematurely deployed his parachute. That led to a violent collision between McRaven and the unfurling chute. This impact left him disoriented, prompting him to swiftly release his own parachute. However, the lines of his parachute became entangled around his legs and caused excruciating strain as they pulled in opposite directions.

As Admiral McRaven told Rachel Martin from NPR, the accident "kind of snapped me in two. So it broke my pelvis several inches apart, ripped muscles out of my stomach and my legs, and fractured my back. I landed about two miles from the drop zone."[v]

Although prompt surgical intervention mended his fractured back and pelvis, McRaven confronted an arduous road to recovery that was marked by many months of enforced inactivity. During this period of convalescence, as he lay confined to a hospital bed within the comfort of his own home, the fateful events of September 11, 2001, unfolded before his eyes.

Witnessing the horrifying attacks on the World Trade Center in New York City and the strike on the Pentagon, McRaven realized the United States was on the precipice of a new era characterized by armed conflict. He understood that the demand for special operations forces would be greater than ever.

McRaven's disciplined spirit refused to yield to his terrible injuries. Within weeks, he defied the odds and was on his feet. Within months, he had reclaimed his operational status.

His journey didn't end there. McRaven went on to achieve remarkable feats, including commanding a squadron in the Naval Special Warfare Development Group; overseeing all special operations in Afghanistan and Iraq; and orchestrating the mission that brought down Osama Bin Laden.

The "return with the elixir" found McRaven sharing the profound lessons of his discipline in his book, *Make Your Bed: Little Things That Can Change Your Life...And Maybe the World*, a literary treasure that has sold over a million copies. His University of Texas commencement address, viewed over fourteen million times on YouTube, inspired countless souls. McRaven's discipline shaped his destiny and ignited the aspirations of millions.

Discipline begins with small things, done correctly over and over again–such as making your bed in the morning. All branches of the military emphasize attention to detail, discipline, and organization; and making the bed each morning is one of the ways to instill these values in service members who come from all walks of life.

For many, making their bed may be a novel experience. It's a simple task that requires consistency and discipline, and by completing it each morning soldiers achieve a small victory that sets a positive tone for the day. This sense of accomplishment can boost their confidence and motivation, encouraging them to tackle more significant challenges. And it also encourages teamwork–recruits quickly learn that to get the job done quickly, it's faster and easier if two people team up and help each other.

What's more, as the admiral pointed out, if you've had a bad day then coming back to a neat and clean bed at night gives you a little boost. It's like starting over with a clean slate.

McRaven's story reminds us that discipline is the catalyst for transformation. It's the bridge that carries us from aspiration to accomplishment, from the ordinary to the extraordinary. With self-discipline, as Theodore Roosevelt wisely said, "most anything is possible."

Power of Self-Discipline

Discipline keeps us going in our pursuit of aspirations and propels us to take consistent action every day. Angela Duckworth's 2011 study showed that self-discipline better predicts academic success among eighth graders than IQ: "The findings suggest a major reason for students falling short of their intellectual potential: their failure to exercise self-discipline."[vi] This study proves that discipline is vital in steering us towards success, even at a young age.

A lack of discipline often stems from a lack of vision. "If you lack discipline, what you really lack is vision." When you have a clear and compelling vision, discipline naturally follows as an offshoot of the desire to achieve the goal.

This insight sheds light on the underlying cause of why some may struggle with discipline; it's not merely a failure to act but a failure to envision a future worth striving for. By focusing on cultivating a strong vision, we lay the groundwork for discipline to flourish, guiding us towards the realization of our goals.

For example: Until age sixteen, **Sir Richard Branson** attended Stowe School, a private school in Buckinghamshire, England. Branson has dyslexia and he had a poor academic performance. On his last day at school the headmaster, Robert Drayson, famously told him he would either end up in prison or become a millionaire.

Branson quickly found his true calling as an entrepreneur. After starting and growing several businesses under the Virgin brand, he became a millionaire in 1973 thanks to the recording of Mike

Oldfield's *Tubular Bells* platinum album on Virgin Records. He became a billionaire in 1991 when he sold the record company.

The foundation of discipline lies in our vision for what we want and our passion for getting it. It shapes our mindset and self-talk, influencing how we perceive ourselves and our potential. Nurturing a mindset of determination and persistence enables us to replace negative self-talk with positive affirmations that reinforce our belief in ourselves and our future.

Our brain cannot simultaneously focus on negative and positive thoughts. We need to choose one or the other.

To enhance discipline, we can start small. By setting attainable goals or aspirations and focusing on taking consistent, incremental steps towards them, we gradually develop positive habits, build momentum, and strengthen our discipline over time.

Accountability is another vital element of discipline. Finding someone who can hold us accountable for our actions and provide support in staying on track with our aspirations is invaluable. This person could be a mentor, a coach, a trusted friend, or a family member who can help us stay committed and provide guidance.

When **Jeff Bezos** launched Amazon.com in 1994, two of his major investors were his own parents. They knew it was risky, but it's possible that Jeff was super-determined to succeed precisely because his own parents had backed his venture.

The essence of discipline is also vividly illustrated in Thomas Corley's "Rich Habits" study, which delves deeper into the daily practices of successful individuals. Corley found that eighty-eight percent of wealthy individuals dedicate at least thirty minutes each day to self-education or self-improvement reading, emphasizing discipline as a cornerstone of their success.

This rigorous commitment to personal growth and learning is a testament to how disciplined habits can lead to wealth and achievement. The study exemplifies that discipline extends beyond mere financial success; it encompasses a lifestyle of continuous learning and self-improvement.

Discipline is about mastering self-control and maintaining focus on our commitments, even in the face of challenges. By adopting a disciplined mindset and engaging in regular, focused actions, we build the resilience, self-confidence, and determination needed for success. Whether it's through setting small, achievable goals, seeking accountability from mentors or peers, or committing to lifelong learning, the journey of discipline is a transformative process that shapes our destiny.

Thomas Corley's insights serve as a powerful reminder of the profound impact disciplined habits can have on our lives, reinforcing the idea that with discipline most anything is possible.

Stay True to Your Commitments

A wise mentor once asked me, "What does it take to succeed? What do you have to do?"

Wanting to sound smart, I listed a dozen keys to success.

After hearing my responses, he smiled and said, "The answer is simple: To be successful, say what you're going to do, and when, and then do it–no excuses."

My mentor's advice is a powerful principle for crafting a life of integrity, focus, and empowerment. Make a decision and trust yourself to follow through. Honoring commitments builds self-trust and the trust of others.

Much negative self-talk is around breaking trust or promises with ourselves. We beat ourselves up when we don't honor our commitments.

Imagine the guy who tells himself he won't get drunk again, only to stop at the bar on the way home the next day. Or the woman who says she is committed to building her business, but quits at the first "no" she gets. These people don't trust themselves to do what they say they will do. There is power in making a decision once and then trusting yourself!

What would it mean to you if you could fully trust yourself to make a decision once and then follow through? What goals would you set if you knew you would take consistent action to accomplish them? How much confidence would you gain if you knew you kept your word to yourself and your promises to others? Having the discipline to keep your promises is a lifeline in a world cluttered with demons and distractions that can divert us from achieving our dreams.

Distractions are the enticing, immediate gratifications that pull us away from our longer-term aspirations. Just as discipline anchors us in our vision, distractions sever that tether, leaving us adrift in a sea of fleeting whims and momentary pleasures. The danger of distraction lies not only in its immediate diversion but in its potential to become habitual. Just as consistent action strengthens discipline, regular indulgence strengthens distraction. Over time, yielding to distractions can erode our discipline and create a chasm between us and our goals.

Blitz actions are an excellent antidote to prolonged distractions. They break the cycle, refocus our energies, and offer a refreshing intensity that reignites our passion and discipline. Just as a laser beam can cut through the densest material because of its focused intensity, Blitz actions can pierce the haze of distractions and bring clarity and direction.

Both discipline and distraction are cultivated through consistent actions over time. The neurological channels become engraved ever more deeply in our brain, like rivers carving their way through a landscape. While discipline aligns us with our wholesome vision and long-term aspirations, distractions pull us towards the habitual pursuit of short-lived pleasures–often at the cost of our larger goals. We can nurture and strengthen our discipline by understanding the nature of distractions and using tools, including Blitz actions, to break their cycle.

Rafael Nadal: Disciplined Action

The life of tennis great **Rafael Nadal** embodies the epitome of discipline in action.

In a career-defining moment, Rafael Nadal faced Roger Federer in the Wimbledon finals in 2008. The crowd was electric, the tension palpable. Federer, then the reigning king of tennis, had already won twelve Grand Slam titles. Nadal, though formidable, was considered a clay court specialist. The stakes were monumental for the title and for Nadal's identity in tennis.

For hours, they dueled in the most extended Wimbledon final in history. The fifth and final set was a seismic shift in energy. Nadal's left knee was virtually screaming with pain, a reminder of the relentless tendonitis that had plagued him. Sweat dripped down his face like a broken faucet. His stutter as a child seemed minor in comparison to this crucible. But every excruciating rally was fueled by years of disciplined action: the countless hours on clay courts in Mallorca, the strict daily regimens, the meticulous analysis of opponents' gameplay.

When Nadal finally clinched the last point after 4 hours and 48 minutes, the world witnessed the crowning of a new Wimbledon champion and the metamorphosis of a man who had confronted his most daunting obstacle yet. His win broke Federer's five-year Wimbledon winning streak and proved that Nadal wasn't just a clay-court phenomenon.

He had the *vision* to build his championship castle. He *believed* he could do it. He set his *priorities* on winning. He created the necessary *environment* to make it happen. And he had the *discipline* to see it through to the end, catapulting him into the ranks of the all-time greats.

Since that iconic match, Nadal's career has been a litany of astonishing achievements. With fourteen French Open titles and twenty-two Grand Slam singles titles, by 2023 he was second to Djokovic for the most in men's history. His mental fortitude is credited with a winning percentage of eighty-three percent in Grand Slam matches, a stat that underscores the strength of his disciplined approach.

The Essence of Victory: Discipline as the Foundation of Success. Nadal's Wimbledon win wasn't a fluke; it was the natural outcome of a life defined by disciplined action. His journey underscores the transformative power of discipline in navigating life's most daunting challenges. With discipline, not even the sky is the limit–it's another milestone to conquer.

Critical Strategies for Disciplined Action

In order to take disciplined action, you need clear, specific, and measurable goals. Break them into smaller milestones to create a roadmap for action and enhance your focus and determination. Incorporating actions and controllables into your plan ensures that your goals are not just visionary, but actionable. This involves identifying steps that are within your control and committing to them. Creating actionable plans empowers you to take focused action and measure your progress. Commit to taking consistent action. Small, consistent efforts accumulate over time to yield significant results. Minimum and Standard actions represent the small stones that, when piled up over time, build the strong walls and five towers of your castle.

The threads that connect every success story are universal: resilience, purpose, vision, and discipline. When you face a challenge and think you can't push through, but somehow you do, you feel euphoric! That's the power of self-belief and discipline. Self-discipline is neither a burden nor a chore. It's a bridge, a catalyst, and a choice. Choose discipline, choose growth, and let your story inspire others, as Sara Hodgen did.

Leading Your Ideal Life

In a recent mastermind group, I met **Sara Hodgen**. A few months later sent me an incredible email. With her permission, I share what Sara had to say:

#

Life can be complicated, and I often found myself anxious about how I could fit all that was required of me twenty-four hours a day. I also kept worrying if I was impacting the areas that mattered most. I felt pulled in many directions without much guidance on where to focus.

I was lost when I started my business, as I was new to the industry. I work full-time, have two busy teenagers, am a wife, a chef, a house cleaner, and a taxi driver. I had a buffet, not a plate, was winging it and felt pulled in many directions. I was confused about what to do each day but knew that I needed to do something. When I would focus on one priority, others fell short or were put on the back burner.

I overcome this obstacle by investing my time (the little that I had!) in personal and professional development. I attended my first Breakthrough Workshop, aka The Mini Mastermind, with Rob Sperry in Coeur d'Alene, ID. This is where I first heard of the castle concept and was determined to get organized. My business was all that I focused on and processed as I listened to Rob teaching about Minimums, Standards, and Blitzes.

Brilliant idea! What a way to perform non-negotiables, even on my worst days ever, set a Standard "regular day," and then Blitz on some days when I am running full steam ahead. It was easy for me to identify business-related actions since at that time that is where my focus needed to be.

My mindset was laser-focused on my business, and I blocked out other things on my agenda that mattered. When I returned home, I started on my business habits. I quickly found that in doing so, other things continued to be left undone: relationships were not as strong as they could be, and my health was being sacrificed, leading to still feeling pulled in many directions.

I trusted the process and kept going, but was so frustrated that other areas of my life were falling apart, and I didn't know what to do. Then, I went to Oceanside, CA, for the mastermind where Rob spoke again about the castle concept. This time it clicked! I was missing something, a massive part of my castle that I failed to make a priority. Talk about an ah-ha moment! Was it because I was in the thick of burnout mode from only focusing on my business and not my other priorities? Absolutely!

Bring on identifying and being intentional in all the priorities that matter to me, with establishing Minimums, Standards, and Blitzes, too! Creating my castle, mapping out my action list, keeping track of my progress, and sticking to it have worked wonders in ensuring my castle doesn't crumble with all my priorities at the top.

Before I heard of creating my castle, ***my vision was unclear***, and I was flying by the seat of my pants with no plan. Demons seemed to swarm from every direction. It absolutely helps me excel in my business, but that's not all that defines me and my castle. Creating my castle with all my priorities at the top helped me to identify the areas in my life that were often put on the back burner and that I was sacrificing for my business. The game changed when my mind shifted to working on all priority areas. With a ***clear vision*** of my castle, peace, and clarity were found in knowing that the structure was intact daily and harmony within its walls.

#

I'm thankful to Sara for allowing me to share her story with you. It beautifully demonstrates the importance of having a clear and compelling vision that is equipped with a roadmap, and having the motivation to turn that vision into reality.

The capacity to change is available to you, too. However, you need a clear vision of what you want to achieve and where you want to be–your desired future state or dream castle–so you can create an environment that propels you towards your goals and allows you to enjoy sustainable success.

Imagine your life as a blank canvas, where every stroke of your brush paints the story you wish to tell. Every color, every shade, is yours to choose. Or imagine your life as a book and your future as blank pages. Your story is still being written. You hold the pen and the pages ahead are brimming with potential. I invite you to create more memories, chase your dreams, and celebrate the beautiful journey and scenic destinations. May you always find the courage to chase your dreams, the strength to take action, and the wisdom to cherish every moment.

Your ideal life is within your grasp. Please do not leave it to chance. You can design and create your own castle, your ideal life.

Craft your own clear and compelling vision. And then set Minimum, Standard, and Blitz actions to progress towards your dream castle. Beware of internal and external demons that seek to disrupt your life and destroy your castle! Creating your desired life is an ongoing journey punctuated by storms and challenges, but I assure you: You can die with many happy memories, not unfulfilled dreams!

AFTERWORD

CASTLES IN THE AIR

This book will help you build them

By Ken Shelton

For six decades I have enjoyed the writing of Henry David Thoreau, the American essayist who once wrote:

> *"If you have built castles in the air, your work need not be lost; that is where they should be. Now put the foundations under them."*

If ever a person strived to put foundations under dream castles it would be the author of this book, Rob Sperry. While I have only known him since January 2024, I have known his family for six decades–and they are all builders of castles with firm foundations.

Familiar with the Sperry Family Legacy

Over six decades, you become very familiar with an author or a family.

Growing up in Provo, Utah, I often encountered the imposing figure of **Sidney B. Sperry**. He is considered to be the father of religious education at Brigham Young University, perhaps its first full-fledged biblical scholar, who singlehandedly transformed its religious education and served as a mentor to every dean of Religious Education for five decades. He had the rare attributes of humility and unshakable faith, and he was the great-grandfather of our author, Rob Sperry.

I once met **Sidney L. Sperry**, the eldest son of Sidney B. Sperry. He was a Navy veteran of World War II and served in the South Pacific. At Texas Christian University he was on the swim team, played center on the basketball team, and played tight-end on the football team. He was also an avid tennis enthusiast. He graduated from BYU and there founded the Sidney B. Sperry Symposium. This was the grandfather of our author, Rob Sperry.

I have long known **Rob Sperry**, the father of Rob Sperry, author of this book; in fact, I have been in his home many times and visited with him and his wife Annette. I admired how they live and lead their circumspect lives and attend to their home, family and business. For many years Rob was a well-respected tennis coach at Timpview High School in Provo, Utah, where his teams won several state titles.

In January 2024 I met **Rob Sperry**, author of this book, through a mutual friend, Dan McCormick, at my home in Provo. I quickly realized the truth of the Proverb: "The apple does not fall far from the tree," meaning a child often grows up to be similar to its parents both in behavior and in physical characteristics. In this case, that's a good thing–if you care about building castles and creating a life of meaning, joy, fulfillment, and success.

How Rob Builds CASTLES

In this book, Rob identified what robs many people of their dreams–things like demons and distractions–and he offers a remedy, **seven actions** that will empower us to gain and sustain what we envision to be success in life. To help me remember the actions, I created this acronym:

Clear *Vision*

Attitude and *Belief*

Select *Priorities*

Take *Action*

Log *Win Streaks*

En*vironment*

Sustain with *Discipline*

If you are like me, you are likely frustrated with your attempts at castle building. You start, but then stop. You are dedicated and committed, but then get distracted. You have pure intent, but you are beset by demons. You have the resolve, but you lack resources. And so on. With Rob's Castle System, you eliminate the *ifs, ands, and buts*. You just do it, a little at a time.

Why Proactive People Prosper

Proactive people tend to prosper because they begin with small steps and a clear vision or a compelling end in mind. They put first things first. They are not reactionary victims of their conditions, conditioning and circumstances. They overcome debilitating addictions and dependencies and become independent, and then become interdependent with like-minded team members. They are action-oriented and their actions are aligned with their vision and values. And they sustain progress with discipline and discipleship.

What Rob Sperry Wants for You

This is what Rob Sperry wants for you: Peace, Prosperity, and Abundance. He wants you to die with sweet memories, not with unfulfilled dreams. Yes, he wants you to envision, create, possess, live in and love your own castles.

Ken Shelton has served as editor/publisher of *Leadership Excellence* and *Personal Excellence* magazines and books for thirty years. He was ghostwriter for Stephen R. Covey on two books: *The 7 Habits of Highly Effective People* and *Principle-Centered Leadership*.

He is the author of *Field Leadership, Beyond Counterfeit Leadership,* and twelve other books. In 2015, the World Leadership Congress presented him with the Global Business Leadership Excellence Award.

ABOUT THE AUTHOR

Rob Sperry is an internationally recognized leader, coach, trainer, consultant, author, speaker and entrepreneur. He has been featured in several publications, books, podcasts, blogs, articles, and magazines. As a speaker, he has addressed audiences in twenty-three countries.

He now spends his time traveling the world speaking, training, hosting mastermind retreats, and enjoying family life with his wife Janei'a and their four amazing children Cade, Kaia, Kiri, and Ren.

As crazy as it sounds, most people never leave reviews when they love a good book. It would mean a lot to me if you would take the time to leave a review on Amazon.

Endnotes

i. https://www.apa.org/pubs/journals/releases/psp-pspa0000363.pdf

ii. https://ics.uci.edu/~gmark/chi08-mark.pdf

iii. https://www.pcma.org/open-office-spaces-distractions-noise/

iv. NYT. https://www.nytimes.com/2007/07/25/health/25iht-fat.4.6830240.html

v. NPR. https://www.npr.org/2019/06/25/735638003/william-mcravens-sea-stories-my-life-in-special-operations

vi. Duckworth AL, Seligman ME. Self-discipline outdoes IQ in predicting academic performance of adolescents. Psychol Sci. 2005 Dec;16(12):939-44. doi: 10.1111/j.1467-9280.2005.01641.x. PMID: 16313657.